Doctoring While Female

DOCTORING WHILE FEMALE

THE PERSONAL AND NATIONAL TOLL OF GENDER INEQUITY IN MEDICINE

KOLLEEN CANNON DOUGHERTY
MD, FASA

HOUNDSTOOTH
PRESS

COPYRIGHT © 2025 KOLLEEN CANNON DOUGHERTY
All rights reserved.

DOCTORING WHILE FEMALE
The Personal and National Toll of Gender Inequity in Medicine

FIRST EDITION

ISBN 978-1-5445-4905-7 *Hardcover*
       978-1-5445-4904-0 *Paperback*
       978-1-5445-4903-3 *Ebook*

To Stinky, Ellis, Frazier, Harry, and Tessa.

And, of course, Maizie Mae, Jamie JuJu, and ZuZu.

You are my why!

Love you more!

Mu

CONTENTS

AUTHOR'S NOTE 9
WOMEN'S PATH TO PROGRESS 11
PREFACE 17
INTRODUCTION 19

1. PLANTING A SEED 29
2. EQUAL BUT NOT EQUAL 37
3. THE PLAYING FIELD IS MALE 53
4. A NAME IS JUST A NAME, OR IS IT? 63
5. PERKY AS A JOB REQUIREMENT (IF FEMALE) 71
6. THE TIGHTROPE, OR THE LIKABILITY CONUNDRUM 77
7. THE MOTHERHOOD TAX 87
8. DEMOTION AS NEUTRALIZATION 101
9. ECHOES OF DISCONTENT 119
10. THE FINAL STRAW 127
11. THE MURKY MIDDLE 137
12. VICTORY BUT WALKING WOUNDED 147
13. RECALIBRATION, REDIRECTION, AND REDEFINITION 163
14. WOMAN VERSUS WOMAN 173

15. TAKE UP SPACE AND USE YOUR VOICE 183
16. THE BIG PICTURE 191
17. LESSONS LEARNED AND MOVING FORWARD 201

CONCLUSION... 215
AFTERWORD.. 219
ACKNOWLEDGMENTS... 225
FRAMEWORKS AND CONCEPTS INDEX............................... 229
EXTENDED READING 235
ABOUT THE AUTHOR.. 239
NOTES 241

AUTHOR'S NOTE

"There is never regret in doing your best, which is all any of us can really do. Even if you fail, you'll feel at ease knowing that it wasn't due to the lack of trying."
—WIDELY ATTRIBUTED TO LAURA PUNSU

This book is an honest attempt to share my story of becoming a doctor, practicing as a doctor, and surviving being a woman in the male-dominated field of doctoring. It is also an attempt to share thoughts, some coming to me retrospectively, on how to make the workplace better and to move women further along the path to equity.

In my attempts to capture the events of my life, I have looked through countless personal journals, emails, calendars and day planners, work schedules and notes; relistened to audiotapes; conducted interviews; and dove deep into research and data. I have purposely left out names and identifying characteristics of colleagues, especially given the unflattering light they might be shed under. When needed, I have approximated dialogue, to the best of my memory. I have taken great care in this endeavor to share my truth of what happened throughout my journey as a physician.

This is my story, how I remember it, and how it has affected me and those around me.

WOMEN'S PATH TO PROGRESS

While this book centers primarily on my personal journey, interspersed with statistics and analytical frameworks, it's also essential to place my experiences within the broader historical narrative of women's struggles in the workplace and, more specifically, in medicine. My story is one of many, but it reflects a relatively recent chapter in the ongoing battle for gender equality. Women have long fought to break through barriers in traditionally male-dominated fields, and the challenges I've encountered are both deeply personal and part of a much larger, evolving story of discrimination, resilience, and progress.

The Women in the Workplace and at Home timeline underscores how women have had to navigate societal expectations, often torn between professional ambitions and domestic responsibilities. World War II ushered women into the workforce to fill the void in the job market left by men drafted into the war, but the postwar era reinforced rigid gender roles. The second wave of feminism, with landmark moments like the publication of *The Feminine Mystique* and the passage of reproductive rights, spotlighted women's growing dissatisfaction with these constraints. These shifts have directly impacted female physicians, who, in addition to medical challenges, face the burden of societal expectations regarding their roles as caregivers and professionals.

These historical contexts are directly related to the challenges I've faced at work. The scarcity mindset, internalized misogyny, and tokenism that I've observed in the workplace are part of the larger struggle women have faced in gaining equal footing in male-dominated environments. Understanding this historical foundation provides crucial insight into the frustrations I've encountered: the competition among women, the lack of support, and the expectation to prove oneself in a space still not designed for women to thrive equitably.[1]

I also wanted to zoom in on women in the medical workplace in history. The Women in Medicine timeline highlights the critical contributions women have made to medical research and patient care throughout history, reinforcing the undeniable fact that women have always been present in the field. From Elizabeth Blackwell's trailblazing achievement as the first female physician in the US to Dr. Katalin Karikó's work on the COVID-19 vaccine, these milestones reveal how women have not only shaped medicine but have revolutionized it in ways that benefit society as a whole. Yet even with these groundbreaking contributions, the persistent underrepresentation in leadership and the pay gap underscore how systemic discrimination still plagues the field today.

For women like me who have experienced misogyny and discrimination firsthand in the medical field, the historical struggle for equity is not just a backdrop but an ongoing reality. The timelines illustrate how far we've come in terms of female representation and autonomy, but they also highlight the systemic challenges that remain—especially in fields like medicine, where women's contributions continue to be undervalued and underrepresented at the leadership level. These societal dynamics, laid bare by history, remind us that the fight for equality is ongoing and that continued advocacy for systemic change is critical for future generations.

WOMEN IN THE WORKPLACE & AT HOME IN RECENT US HISTORY

1848
1st wave feminism
It started at the Seneca Falls Convention and focused on women's sufferage, property rights, and legal inequalities.

1919
19th amendment
The amendment gave women the right to vote.

1941-1945
WWII—women enter the workforce
Women were encouraged to work in factories, offices, and other jobs to fill roles left vacant by men who went to fight in the war. "Rosie the Riveter" became a symbol of female empowerment during this era, as millions of women took on jobs that were previously considered male-only.

1945-1950s
post-WWII gender roles
After WWII, men returned from the war and resumed their jobs, while women were encouraged to leave the workforce and return to homemaking. The image of the ideal American woman in the 1950s was one who was a wife and mother, often seen wearing pearls, cooking dinner, and living behind a white picket fence. However, this ideal was not attainable for many, especially poor women and women of color, who had to balance both work and home responsibilities.

1963
***The Feminine Mystique* by Betty Friedan**
This book became a catalyst for the 2nd wave of feminism. It articulated the frustrations many women felt at being confined to homemaker roles and sparked a movement that focused on women's rights beyond voting, particularly in education, work, and reproductive rights.

1964
gender added to CRA
The Civil Rights Act of 1964 initially aimed to address racial discrimination. However, gender discrimination was also added to the bill. This was a crucial moment in the fight for workplace equality and anti-discrimination protections for women.

1965
***Griswold v. CT*—right to family planning**
SCOTUS decision ruled that married couples had the right to use contraception based on the right to privacy. A turning point for reproductive rights, this paved the way for greater access to family planning options and gave women more autonomy over their bodies and lives.

1972
Equal Rights Act introduced
The ERA, which sought to guarantee equal rights regardless of sex, was passed by Congress in 1972 and sent to the states for ratification. The amendment had a ten-year deadline for ratification, but despite significant advocacy, it fell short of the necessary 38 state approvals by the 1982 deadline. The fight for the ERA continues to this day.

1973
***Roe v. Wade*—abortion rights**
SCOTUS decision legalized abortion nationwide, recognizing a woman's right to choose as part of her right to privacy under the Constitution. This decision became a landmark case for reproductive rights and remains a highly debated issue.

1993
Family & Medical Leave Act
This act guaranteed 12 weeks of unpaid leave for certain family and medical reasons, providing a crucial step in helping women balance careers and family life.

2009
Lilly Ledbetter Fair Pay Act
Signed into law by President Obama, this act made it easier for employees to challenge pay discrimination, addressing persistent gender wage gaps in the workforce.

2010
#MeToo movement
The #MeToo movement against sexual harassment and assault gained national and international prominence, sparking widespread awareness of workplace discrimination and gendered violence.

2022
Dobbs decision
SCOTUS *Dobbs v. Jackson Women's Health Organization* overturned the 1973 *Roe v. Wade* decision, eliminating the constitutional right to abortion, sparking renewed activism and protests across the country.

PRESENT
gender pay gap & leadership representation
The gender pay gap continues to affect women today, but the disparities are even more pronounced for women of color. While white women earn about 79 cents for every dollar earned by white men, Black women earn around 70 cents, Latina women about 65 cents, and Native American women just 60 cents. Leadership representation shows similar disparities: white women hold 10.4% of Fortune 500 CEO roles, whereas women of color make up less than 1%.

PRESENT
intersectional feminism
The feminist movement today emphasizes intersectionality, recognizing that race, class, sexual orientation, and other identities shape women's experiences. Activism focuses on reproductive justice, trans rights, LGBTQ+ inclusion, and dismantling systemic inequalities.

WOMEN IN MEDICINE
We have and will always be here!

1847
Elizabeth Blackwell admitted to med school
Elizabeth Blackwell became the first woman admitted to a US medical school (Geneva Medical College, NY), earning her medical degree in 1849 and paving the way for women in American medicine.

1864
Rebecca Lee Crumpler graduates med school
Rebecca Lee Crumpler was the first African American woman to receive a Medical Degree (MD) in the United States. She challenged the prejudice that prevented African Americans and women from pursuing medical careers.

1914
Marie Curie & X-ray technology
Although primarily known for her work in physics and chemistry, she was instrumental in developing X-ray technology for medical purposes during World War I, allowing for faster diagnosis and treatment of injuries.

1944
Dr. Helen Brooke Taussig founds pediatric cardiology
Dr. Taussig, a founder of pediatric cardiology, developed the first surgical treatment for "blue baby syndrome," revolutionizing pediatric heart care.

1947
Gerty Cori wins Nobel Prize
Gerty Cori became the first woman to win the Nobel Prize in Physiology or Medicine for her pioneering work on carbohydrate metabolism, impacting diabetes research.

1951
Henrietta Lacks's cells become "HeLa"
Without her consent, cells taken from Henrietta Lacks, a Black woman undergoing cancer treatment, were used to create the HeLa cell line. These cells became crucial for numerous medical breakthroughs, including the development of the polio vaccine, cancer treatments, and advances in genetics.

1952
Rosalind Franklin's double helix DNA
Franklin was a key figure in the discovery of the DNA double helix, using X-ray crystallography to capture critical images that led to this groundbreaking understanding of genetics. Although her contributions were underappreciated during her lifetime, her work has since been recognized as pivotal in molecular biology and medical research.

1957
Virginia Apgar develops the Apgar Score
Virginia Apgar created the Apgar Score, a quick assessment tool used to evaluate the health of newborns immediately after birth, revolutionizing neonatal care worldwide.

1979
Rosalyn Yalow's work in radioimmunoassay
Rosalyn Yalow was awarded the Nobel Prize in Physiology or Medicine for her work in radioimmunoassay, a technique that has had a significant impact on hormone testing and medical research.

1984
Elizabeth Blackburn discovers telomerase
Elizabeth Blackburn, an Australian-American biologist, was awarded the Nobel Prize for her discovery of the enzyme telomerase, which has significant implications for cancer research and aging.

1993
NIH revokes ban on female participants
The NIH reversed its policy excluding women of childbearing age from clinical trials, leading to more inclusive research and addressing gender differences in health outcomes.

2012
Dr. Jennifer Doudna & CRISPR-Cas9
Jenniter Doudna, along with Emmanuelle Charpentier, developed CRISPR-Cas9 gene-editing technology, transforming genetic research and its potential applications in medicine.

WOMEN IN MEDICINE cont.
We have and will always be here!

2020
women make up majority of US medical school students
For the first time in history, women comprised the majority of US medical school students. According to the Association of American Medical Colleges (AAMC), 50.5% of medical students were women in 2019-2020.

PRESENT
Women in medicine now
Women in medicine face a persistent pay gap, earning about 25-30% less than their male counterparts, even when accounting for factors like speciality and work hours. They also experienced higher rates of burnout, often due to work-life balance struggles and emotional labor, leading to more frequent turnover and early career exits. Despite these challenges, women continue to make vital contributions to the field and advocate for greater equity.

2020
Dr. Katalin Karikó & the COVID-19 vaccine
Dr. Katalin Karikó is a Hungarian-American biologist whose groundbreaking work in mRNA technology was crucial to the rapid development of COVID-19 vaccines, specifically the Pfizer-BioNTech and Moderna vaccines.

2022
women make up 36% of practicing US physicians
As of 2022, women represented 36% of practicing physicians in the US. Despite this progress, women remain underrepresented in leadership positions, with only about 18% of hospital CEOs and 16% of medical school deans being female.

PREFACE

Medicine is a man's world. It was designed by men, for men, and it's run by men. I entered medicine assuming I'd learned the foundations of a promising medical career in medical school. No one teaches you about the unconscious and conscious biases that will determine your career trajectory. I have practiced for over two decades as an anesthesiologist and a critical care intensivist. Both worlds are high-stakes areas where men have ruled.

As a white, blond female in my early thirties, I naively entered the workforce, and boy, was it an eye-opener. Constantly being called by my first name as my male counterparts were addressed by the "doctor" title—called "nurse," "babe," and "blondie" more times than I can count—deepened my sense of non-belonging.

This is my story of traversing that environment, rising to higher levels of power, only to be taken down by a "good old Southern white boy" who believed that women should be "perky," that gender discrimination doesn't exist, and that women don't attain success because they take themselves out of the running by having babies.

Ultimately, armed with lawyers, misogynistic emails, and incriminating audiotapes, a hospital investigation ensued.

This is my story of taking back my power and ultimately the direction of my life.

INTRODUCTION

"I raise my voice not so I can shout, but so that those without a voice can be heard...we cannot succeed when half of us are held back."

—MALALA YOUSAFZAI[2]

This book—what is its purpose? Is it a call to action? Is it meant to galvanize women to work together to raise awareness around biases that limit our full potential? Is it a story about pivoting and finding the strength to walk away from environments that are so toxic and dehumanizing? Is it a story of retribution and how to hold accountable those who foster inequity?

I think it is all these things. It is my story of being put down and held back. Being marginalized, not being valued, and not being compensated equally compared with younger men in my group. It is my story of twenty-four-plus years of microaggressions and belittling comments. It is my story of twenty-four years of a million little cuts that eventually drained me of my joy. It is my story of awakening, realizing that enough was enough, and moving through all my fears, especially the fear of retaliation, which certainly happened. It is my story of overcoming my own limiting beliefs and knowing that I could help by bringing to light this toxic environment and addressing system-wide gaps that help perpetuate the status quo.

This is my story of rising up, reclaiming power over my future, and not letting male "leaders" stifle me. This is also a story for all the women who continue to forge their paths daily, who continue to struggle to find their way around the biases that confront them. Some women cannot leave their jobs because of economic insecurity, and this book is for them, to give them strategies to navigate the misogynistic waters. I realize that I am in a privileged position: because of my age, where I am at in my career trajectory, because I have worked at a high-earning career for two decades and have had a dual-income family, and because I have a supportive husband. I have the luxury to take on this challenge that many women cannot because they need to work to support themselves and their families or because of the astronomical cost of hiring an attorney who can fight a company or hospital with much deeper pockets. I know of women at my same institution and women in other parts of the country, and I am absolutely sure there are women around the world, who have dealt with or who are still dealing with harassment and discrimination. Many women cannot risk losing their job or their income source to fight the fight. This book is for them, to let them know I see them and want more for them.

Why now? Why me? Let's just say I got tired of being called "Blondilocks." Blondilocks was my nickname, given to me by one of my best friends in my group. It was meant to be funny—a play on words. Me, sporting blond hair and, I suppose, in his opinion, being clueless at times. It originated one day when I was unable to perform some computer task, a slide presentation download or something. I honestly cannot remember. I freely admit tech is not my thing. I love it for some things, like copying and pasting rather than having to retype letters and articles like we had to with good old-fashioned typewriters. (Yes, I'm that old. My college applications were all done on a typewriter. Yikes, do kids these days even know what typewriters look like?) But I digress. OK, computer tech is not my thing. But give me a patient suffering from ARDS (adult respiratory distress syndrome), and I can magically fine-tune their ventilator to maximize ventilation and minimize barotrauma. We all have strengths and weaknesses, right?

Well, after an embarrassing attempt at PowerPoint, I called my friend for assistance and came away with the moniker Blondilocks. At first, it seemed like a term of endearment. A joke between friends. But then, in the middle of the OR (operating room), being called that and having the story recounted to others, it seemed less than flattering. But nevertheless, I now have been called "Blondilocks" for twenty-four years.

So back to the question, why now? It was a combination of things: being passed over for promotions while my less-experienced male partners and colleagues were elevated, watching my female colleagues being treated differently, having their authority questioned, and receiving backhanded comments about their perceived—yet unfounded—lack of dedication to their profession and patients because of motherhood. I grew weary of the different standards for men and women. Women consistently have to prove themselves to a greater extent than men to even be recognized.

The good old boys club is alive and well in medicine. It's insidious. Some of the hospital banter might have been said in good fun, but it unconsciously reinforces a male culture that is pervasive and keeps women from being fully let into the inner circle. The gendered language (such as "manpower"), the comments on the appearance of applicants, the mansplaining, the "hepeating," and the marginalization all to keep women in their place.

Many female residents and attendings early in their careers would come to me asking, "How'd you do it?" and "How'd you put up with this for so long?"

Perhaps I was ignorant of the subtleties. I wanted to fit in. I wanted to be accepted in a man's world, the operating room. I knew speaking out was not going to rub people the right way. I also brushed it aside like so many do. Oh, they didn't mean anything by it. It was said in jest. The proverbial "boys will be boys."

Perhaps I needed twenty-four years of it to open my eyes.

Well, "Blondilocks" no more.

I finally realized that allowing all those comments, those dismissals of me and my thoughts, the interruption of women as they are speaking, the lack of promotion, and the lack of resource allocation to females was not affecting just me but all women. It allowed the status quo of medicine, the good old boys club, to remain the same—where you are more likely to become a chair of a department in an academic institution in the United States if you have a mustache than if you are female (at least, as of 2015).[3]

I had had it. Enough was enough.

When I received a departmental email depicting an upside-down snowman with his eyes and carrot nose resembling male genitalia with a caption referring to it, I knew I owed it to all the strong women who initially pioneered into medicine and forged a path for me. I also owed it to all the amazing female colleagues I'd helped train or who would be joining the ranks of this noble profession in the years to come.

I want those women who are embarking on their beginning

stages of their medical journeys to not have to go through what I and every woman who is practicing medicine today has gone through. I want every woman to truly be included, not to be a "token" female on a panel or committee but the fierce contributor and expert that she is. I want every female physician to achieve the career goals that she desires without having to "play the game" and hope that she is the one picked for promotion.

Medicine is hurting. Female physicians are hurting. Female physician burnout is a national epidemic. In June 2023, the article "Gender Differences in Physician Burnout: Driving Factors and Potential Solutions" reported that women physicians generally face heavier workloads, including spending extra time on electronic health records and more time per patient. They also tend to have fewer resources and less control over their schedules and workloads. The lack of women in leadership; pay disparities; limited career progression; and frequent exposure to gender bias, microaggressions, and harassment are significant factors contributing to burnout disparities. Furthermore, women physicians often juggle additional responsibilities outside of work, such as childcare and elder care, which can reduce satisfaction with work-life balance. Lower self-compassion and feelings of being underappreciated also contribute to lower professional fulfillment and higher burnout rates among women in the medical field.[4] These problems were exacerbated by COVID-19. Women are no longer willing to be marginalized, ostracized, and silenced at work. Often, rather than fighting a male-dominated field, they will just leave.[5]

All of this is to say that women physicians leave medicine earlier in their careers compared to their male counterparts, even pre-pandemic. In October 2019, the AAMC (Association of American Medical Colleges) reported that nearly 40 percent of women physicians choose to either reduce their hours to part-time or leave the medical profession entirely within six years of finishing their residency.[6] "When you invest more than a decade of your life to learn a skill and you're willing to walk away from that early in your career, that's more than a red flag. It's a burning fire," said Sasha Shillcutt, MD, professor in the department of anesthesiology at the University of Nebraska Medical Center and founder of Brave Enough, a master class on reducing burnout for women in medicine.[7]

They are unwilling to deal with the chauvinism, discrimination, and, at times, misogyny. Current statistics show that beginning in 2019, 50 percent of incoming medical class students are female.[8] Yet if they retire early, it will exacerbate the already projected physician shortage. It will become a national healthcare crisis.

The American people need those female physicians.

Enter the Goldilocks dilemma. Have you heard of it? The porridge is too hot or too cold. The bed is too soft or too hard. Women are often perceived in a similar way: too tough, strict, and stern—essentially, too masculine—or too soft, submissive, and quiet. Female leaders find themselves critiqued both for being "too feminine" and "too masculine." The tightrope. The catch-22. The Goldilocks dilemma!

In the workplace and hospital boardrooms, it looks a little bit like this: In meetings when a woman raises an issue—call allocation, for example—she is often labeled as a "whiner" or a "complainer." If a man raises the same issue, he often is seen as advancing a legitimate cause. Same exact words, interpreted through the lens of societal behavioral expectations. A woman should stay quiet, be in the kitchen, barefoot and pregnant, and leave the negotiating and problem-solving to the men. If she doesn't, she's a rabble-rouser. Unfortunately, staying quiet also penalizes a woman for advancement. Then she is meek and not seen as a thought leader or able to navigate issues. Classic catch-22.

The following chapters in this book detail my experiences with these types of complications. They detail how I dreamed of being a doctor since I was a little girl, my journey through med school, and what I faced in my workplace for twenty-four years. They detail the catch-22, the emotional toll of being bypassed, the mansplaining, the exclusion, the misogynistic comments, the changes when I became a mother, the demotions, the retaliations, the isolation, the lawsuit, the consequences of my actions. And the gaslighting. Having others pretend that it is your issue and *not* the system. Second-guessing myself. "Did that really happen?"

But this book also details the hope I have for the future of medicine. It details how patients receive better care in the hands of a female physician. It details how we can make the system more equitable for everyone. It details the joy I experienced as a physician, caring for patients and their families at some of their darkest hours. It details where I'm going after being a practicing physician. It details the solidarity, the empowerment, and the love and hope that I have for this industry. Because, ultimately, I'm writing this story not only for me but also to help empower all those who come after me.

MANY READERS MAY WONDER WHETHER THIS WAS ISOLATED TO MY PARTICULAR HOSPITAL OR GROUP. I CAN ASSURE YOU IT IS NOT!

* * *

Unfortunately, gender harassment, discrimination, and inequality are universal. This book is my story in medicine, but unfortunately, this story is retold in all arenas. Women in law, finance, and business all are dealing with this too. My story is one of millions, and it is not even the worst. Many women have suffered much more. But I want to share my truth and hopefully start the conversation.

Medicine, for being an area of innovation and advancement, has not moved the needle very much on this issue. The journal *Academic Emergency Medicine* states that "gender and sexual harassment in academic medicine is persistent and pervasive."[9]

Six in ten medical trainees in emergency medicine have reported gender discrimination or sexual harassment.[10] Fifty-three percent of female faculty and 26 percent of male faculty have experienced some form of gender or sexual harassment in the workplace. Those who experience gender discrimination or sexual harassment suffer negative consequences such as diminished self-confidence and decreased job satisfaction. It also affects institutions with decreased diversity, resulting in adverse consequences for faculty, trainees, and patients as well as increasing staffing turnovers.

Harvard Business Review states that researchers estimate sexual harassment results in an annual productivity loss of about $22,500 for each impacted employee, with many affected individuals experiencing symptoms akin to post-traumatic stress.[11] Due to its detrimental impact on productivity, job satisfaction, organizational commitment, and both physical and mental well-being, it's crucial for managers and organizations to take stronger measures to prevent and eliminate harassment.

Studies have shown that very few people come forward, however, with only 7.6 to 13 percent of trainees who have experienced gender discrimination or sexual harassment reporting it.[12]

THREE QUESTIONS KEPT ARISING IN MY MIND

1. If so few people actually report their experiences, what is the real prevalence of gender discrimination and sexual harassment in medicine?
2. Why are so few willing to report their experiences? What are the barriers?
3. How can we remove the barriers so that the true magnitude of the issue can be seen and therefore addressed?

I wrote this book as part therapy for me as I reflected on all that had happened, as well as part illustrative to others who might be thinking they are alone. I also wrote it to hopefully spark change.

I wanted to share some insights on how women can navigate this male-dominated field and strategies that I wish I had known to mitigate the hurtful sexist comments and put-downs. Lastly, I wanted to share thoughts on what needs to change, system-wide, to allow a more inclusive environment where women are able to thrive and not have to sustain years of microaggressions and macroaggressions.

Can you recognize when you hit rock bottom? We all think we can, or if we got there we could. But what if I told you that most of us may be there, hitting our head against the bottom, but can't see it? We refuse to see it or admit that we are really there. Because then we would have to confront it. We'd have to change, and change is hard. We'd rather stay where we are, even if it's not ideal, because inertia is hard to overcome. It's hard to change. We convince ourselves that it's "not really that bad," or that "he didn't really say that or mean that." We convince ourselves that change would be harder, and we are addicted to comfort. So we stay. We put off making hard choices and decisions, and our indecision is thus our decision to stay. We all do this. Our primitive brain is wired to protect us, and in so doing, it ultimately limits us.

This is ultimately a story of recognizing a toxic environment, deciding I deserve more, and taking control of my life. It's a story of recognizing I had had enough of the put-downs, the marginalization, and the limiting constraints of a male-centric environment. This is my story of Blondilocks no more!

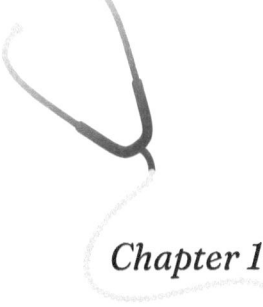

Chapter 1

PLANTING A SEED

"Whatever our dreams, ideas or projects, we plant a seed, nurture it and then reap the fruits of our labor."

—OPRAH WINFREY[13]

I guess I'll just start off by divulging some personal info: I grew up in the 1970s and '80s. That was a time when all the doctors I ever saw were men: my pediatrician, my dentist, my optometrist. When I unfortunately needed nail bed surgery for ingrown toenails (even more personal information) my podiatrist was a man as well. Our dog, Jasper, even went to a male veterinarian when he had a medical issue. Suffice it to say, the world of medicine was male-dominated at that time. And it wasn't just the physicians; when I stepped into any medical office, the pattern was clear: Doctors were men, while nurses, receptionists, hygienists, and support staff were women. I want to be clear: These roles were (and are) vital for keeping these places running efficiently and serving patients. Medicine takes a team, and everyone has a vital role on that team. However, what felt limiting—and what society largely expected—was that women's careers stayed within these supporting roles. Women played essential parts but were rarely seen in the lead. This setup sent a clear message: Women could aim to assist but not to lead. The concept of a female physician never entered my mind until my mother put it there.

This is pretty consistent with what the expectations for women were in the '70s in terms of balancing career and family life—which is to say there wasn't really balance; there was still a huge expectation to give up the former at the expense of the latter. However, this was actively being challenged during my childhood years.

At the beginning of the book, I placed a timeline of US history since the mid-nineteenth century with important dates in regard to women. It's titled Women in the Workplace and at Home in Recent US History. As noted there, dissatisfaction with traditional gender roles and the expectation to be a homemaker was voiced in the early '60s with the publication of *The Feminine Mystique* by Betty Friedan. Several court decisions were made to help women get back into the workforce (from when they held jobs during World War II) with balance in their personal lives (the message pushed on women in the aftermath of the war). These include the *Griswold v. Connecticut* decision, which gave married women the right to contraception and family planning in 1965, and the *Roe v. Wade* decision, which gave women the right to abortion on the basis of privacy in 1973. These legal cases were accompanied by landmark legislation, such as gender being added to the Civil Rights Act of 1964 (which championed equality in the workplace with antidiscrimination clauses) and the Equal Rights Amendment, which was introduced in 1972 and sought to guarantee equal rights regardless of gender on a more general basis. All of this to say: I grew up in the wake of these enactments and a society that was having conversations that challenged stereotypes and social expectations for women. Slowly, more and more women began entering the workforce, challenging the notion that certain jobs were exclusively for men.

I grew up in a stereotypical middle-class family in New Jersey. My father was the hardest-working man ever! For as long as I can remember he had at least two jobs, one in New York City that he commuted over an hour each way to, and on many nights he taught community college computer courses. He also umpired for the community baseball and softball leagues on weekends. While working his two jobs, he put himself through night college. He straddled his college courses around the nights he was not performing his second job. My father was one of five sons, and the first and only in his family to graduate from college. I vividly remember being five years old and standing in the audience on a chair clapping wildly as my father walked across the stage to accept his diploma. My mother, on the other hand, never went to college. She married young, at the age of twenty, which, for the time, was not unusual. She and my father immediately started growing their family and had four children in the next four years. I am the last of the four.

My father's parents lived about an hour north of our house. Unfortunately, my only real memories of my grandfather are after he had his stroke. His stroke confined him to a hospital bed, which took over the entirety of my grandparents' living room. He was quite incapacitated; he could not ambulate or really feed himself. My grandmother cared for him all week long. Every Sunday my mom and dad packed my three siblings and me into our green Ambassador station wagon, and we took an hour's drive north to Fairview, New Jersey. My father mobilized my grandfather into the shower and helped him bathe for the next week. After my dad coiffed my grandfather's thick black-and-gray-speckled hair into a slicked-back do and shaved him, my grandfather was much more ready to greet us. He lacked the core body strength to remain sitting in a chair, so back to bed he went, and the steely cold arm rails petitioned us from him again.

Around the room were family photos, a beautiful picture of my uncle Michael, who was struck by a delivery truck at the age of two and passed way too young. Alongside the photos were different lotions, a bedpan, a urinal, and lots and lots of pills. I wanted so much to help. This was really my first interaction with someone who was sick and who needed care. As we sat next to his railing of his hospital bed in the living room, lots of questions came to my mind. Why couldn't the medicine make it so he could be more like us, active and able to get out of bed? Why did this happen? I knew I wanted to help. My mother whispered to me, "One day you can be a doctor and help people like Grandpa."

I am grateful my mom challenged what she had been taught and what was ingrained into her. My nana was one of fifteen children, the second in line and the oldest girl. Her mother had the herculean job of feeding and clothing her children during the Great Depression. She did not have a complete high school education or a job. She worked in the home, stretching potatoes into a full meal for seventeen (kids and parents together). She had to hand-stitch clothes for the younger children to wear. She converted burlap potato sacks into dresses for the girls.

This is what my nana grew up seeing and role modeling. My mother, too, saw her mom keeping the home. Her aspirations and expectations were to marry after high school, have children, and raise them. That is what she did. No college. No job. She raised me and my siblings. But she also knew there could be more when she casually stated, "Why not be a doctor?" And with that, a casual question, breaking away from the mold of what she had seen, what her subconscious mind told her, she planted a seed in me. A doctor. Yes, that sounded good.

A seed was planted, and inspiration for my future career was born. I wanted to work in the health field. I knew that then. I should just become a doctor. And so there it was. I was going to become a doctor.

I was very fortunate to achieve academic success not only in high school but also in college. I graduated from Emory University in 1986, where I majored in biology and chemistry. With my sights on medical school, I applied to a bunch of schools. I didn't have anyone in my family before me who had gone to medical school, so it was a vast unknown. I applied broadly, some down South, such as the University of Alabama and Vanderbilt (my boyfriend at the time was from Nashville, so that seemed like a good option), and then schools close to my home in New Jersey. I knew med school was going to be challenging, and I thought it would be nice to be closer to home and family support. I applied to my state school, UMDNJ (the Rutgers med school), which seemed the most likely to accept me.

Again, it was my mother who challenged me with a simple question: "What about Columbia?"

Sure, Columbia had a medical school, the Columbia University College of Physicians and Surgeons. It had an extremely low acceptance rate—single digits! Why would they take me?

But my mom quickly responded, "Why not you? They have to take someone. It might as well be you."

So I applied. Reach for the stars!

* * *

I flew home from Georgia, and my dad drove me into the city—Washington Heights, to be exact—across the George Washington Bridge in our green Chevy Chevette. We parked on the corner across from the armory near the Armand Hammer Library, and I walked into the Black Building for my first interview. It was with the head of anatomy, Dr. Ernie April. We drove home after a full day of interviews and tours. I loved everything about the school that day, and I sat wondering what it would be like to learn in New York City and hoping I had impressed them enough for them to grant me one of the coveted spots to be in the class of 1994. Later that year, one day while walking across the campus of Emory, I received my acceptance letter. Columbia accepted me. I did it! It was a surreal moment!

Once again, thanks to my mom, I was inching closer to my dream goal of being a doctor.

To this day, I try to instill into my kids the idea that you need to dream big; you need to take a shot, even if you think the odds or acceptance rates are stacked against you. It reminds me of the Wayne Gretzky quote: "You miss 100 percent of the shots you don't take." You never know unless you try. Put yourself out there, and take a chance on yourself.

If not you, who will?

* * *

After college graduation, I went on to Columbia University College of Physicians and Surgeons and proceeded to have the most exhilarating, challenging, rewarding experiences of my life. Often people ask, "Wasn't medical school horrible?" Later, when I was an intern and resident, colleagues always recounted horror stories of their time in medical school. But not me. I absolutely loved it! I finally was in medical school. I finally was learning all the things I'd hoped to learn, and I was doing it. I was super excited. I also was surrounded by amazing faculty members and an incredible institution, one of the premier centers in the entire United States. I knew that, and I felt it. I cannot say enough about my colleagues, my fellow students of the class of 1994. They were the most amazing group of individuals I have ever met. It's not to say that medical school was easy—the exact opposite—but when you feel like you're living your dream, it's hard to complain.

TAKEAWAYS

1. **Representation shapes your reality:** The examples and role models you encounter profoundly influence your understanding of what is possible.
2. **But your reality can be challenged and reshaped:** Even long-held beliefs or assumptions can be challenged and reshaped by a moment of inspiration or encouragement.
3. **Dream big; act boldly:** Whether through education, career, or personal growth, daring to dream big—and working toward those dreams—can lead to transformative experiences.

CHALLENGES TO YOU

1. **Reflect on your inspirations:** Who planted the seeds that shaped your dreams? Take a moment to think about the pivotal people or moments that inspired you. Write about or share these memories with someone close to you. How did their words or actions change your trajectory?
2. **Examine the seeds you're planting:** Think about the influence you have on others—your family, friends, colleagues, or mentees. Are there ways you can encourage someone to dream bigger? Consider asking thoughtful questions, like my mother did, to help someone see their potential.
3. **Challenge your "Why not me?" moments:** Reflect on moments when you doubted your abilities or decided not to pursue an opportunity because the odds felt slim. Revisit one of those moments, and imagine the outcomes if you had acted differently. How can you apply this reflection to a current goal?
4. **Broaden your role models:** Take stock of the people you admire, whether in your personal life or in the media. Are they diverse in terms of identity, background, or experiences? Seek out stories or biographies of individuals who overcame obstacles to achieve their dreams—they might just plant a seed for your next aspiration.

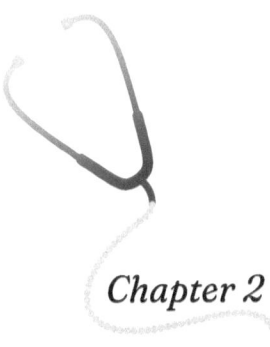

Chapter 2

EQUAL BUT NOT EQUAL

"*The representation of the world, like the world itself, is the work of men; they describe it from their own point of view, which they confuse with absolute truth.*"

—SIMONE DE BEAUVOIR[14]

My first two years at Columbia were an endless array of classes. Anatomy, taught by Dr. April, the same who interviewed me the prior year, was just one of them. Physiology, pharmacology, and histology were also peppered in my schedule. I spent endless nights in the Armand Hammer Library. I found out later the building had nothing to do with baking soda! A huge medical student rite of passage is the iconic moment when they are introduced to their cadavers, all the selfless people who donate their bodies to medical science to help me and all my colleagues learn the intricacies of the human body. In my anatomy group, eight of us crowded around him. To personify him, we gave him a name, Pierre. I'm not really sure why we went with the French name, but it seemed to fit.

The third and fourth years of medical school were clinical rotations. No more heads in our books. No, now we donned our short white coats, differentiated from the longer white attending coats, and joined the hierarchy of medical caregivers to which a patient is subjected. We, though, were the lowest of the low on that hierarchical ladder.

After two years of lectures and examinations, we were finally on the wards. We were seeing patients. We were synthesizing complaints with lab values and physical exam findings to come to a unified thesis and plan of therapy. We were students and learners, taking it all in. We learned from everyone: the patients, our residents, our attendings, the nurses, each other. Every day was different, with different challenges and lots of highs—the first IV successfully placed, the first clinical patient's presentation deemed to be "flawless"—and many lows—missed diagnoses, blown intravenous lines, turning the nasogastric tube from suction to reverse flow. One of my most harrowing experiences was when I thought I almost drowned a patient in his own stomach contents. We were rounding outside a patient's door and my surgical 3 (third-year surgical resident) was leading an afternoon pre-round session before signing out with our attending. He asked me to go turn the patient's NG (nasogastric) suction tube back on. I had seen the lever turned often and thought I knew what I was doing. Obviously not! After I turned the lever 45 degrees, the contents from the wall canister started to quickly flow into him! Instead of sucking his contents out, he was flooded with his gastric juices, causing him to gurgle and be in extremis. Oh, the memories!

Every day I rose, showered, and prepared myself for the day ahead. I walked out of tower 2, apartment 2A, down Haven

Avenue, past the library with its bagel cart promptly parked outside for all the hungry students, and into Milstein pavilion. I met up with my friends and colleagues who were each facing their own mental insecurities as well. We then began to pre-round. It was 5:00 in the morning; the sun had not yet broken through the haze, and we were in charge of collecting all the data on our three patients. This included all the events of the last twenty-four hours, the vitals, the labs, and the consult recommendations. We were synthesizing complaints with lab values and physical exam findings to come to a unified thesis and plan of therapy. We were expected to succinctly present it all on morning rounds in what was called the SOAP note, stating the Subjective, the Objective, the Assessment, and ultimately the Plan for the day. But we were just third-year medical students. We were at Columbia University College of Physicians and Surgeons, and we were in subgroup 3B.

During our surgical rotation, which lasted six weeks, we pre-rounded and then rounded with our residents and attending all before the ORs started and before many rose for their day. After morning rounds were relentless hours of retraction and suction, barely even approaching the operative table. Our retraction was somewhat painful; hours later, in the same position, our hands often felt like they were frozen in a contractured state. Our presence, though menial and painful to us, was integral to aiding those more senior in their heroic attempts to excise, repair, and transform the lives of the patients under their scalpels. It was exciting. We were finally doing something, not just studying.

※ ※ ※

My four years at Columbia are one of the biggest highlights of my life. The classes, learning what I always dreamed about, my classmates, New York City. It was amazing. My class had roughly equal numbers of men and women. We all took anatomy together, struggled to plate slides for the histology lab, crammed all-nighters in the library stacks, and persevered through four years of medical school. We tackled board examinations and matched into internships and residencies across all fields of medicine.

We trained side by side.

Many of us, men and women, equal in all ways.

But we did not have equal prospects.

Even if we had the same board scores, the same evaluations in the same field of study at the same institutions, our prospects were not the same.

Hypothetically, two medical students graduate from the same medical school in the same year and match into the same residency. After completing an internship and residency, both graduate and pass their boards, achieving the same exact grade.

On paper, a curriculum vitae, or a resume, the two graduates are exactly the same.

However, one has a statistically lower chance of becoming an academic professor or departmental chair. The same one is less likely to receive tenure, NIH funding, or research grants and less likely to receive good evaluations or be asked to speak on a panel. The same one will earn 10 percent less per year—which is millions of dollars less over the course of their career—even if working the same number of hours at the same institution.

What is the cause of these differences and different career opportunities?

It is simply their gender. One is male and one female.

PAY GAPS AND OPPORTUNITY GAPS

Throughout a female physician's career, the missed opportunities add up. A 2021 study published in *Health Affairs* found that over the course of a forty-year career, a female physician will typically earn $2 million less than her male counterparts.[15] Christopher Whaley, a policy researcher at the RAND Corporation and lead author of that 2021 study, noted that this is a conservative estimate. A year later, a follow-up reported that this pay gap breaks down to an annual disparity of 25 percent less for women in primary care and 31 percent less for those in specialist roles.[16]

Beyond pay discrepancies, women in medicine encounter several barriers to advancement and recognition. Female physicians are more likely to be evaluated less favorably.[17] They face lower odds of securing professorships or endowed departmental chair positions and are less likely to receive NIH funding.[18] Their research is also less frequently published and cited, which can stymie career growth and impact.[19] Furthermore, female physicians are less likely to be invited to speak at conferences or to participate in expert panels, limiting their visibility and influence in the field. These compounded disparities underscore the structural inequities that continue to hinder women in medicine.[20]

BEYOND MEDICINE AND A DIVE INTO BIASES

Unfortunately, medicine does not have a monopoly on pushing women aside. Other industries and fields similarly have gender imbalances and inherent systems that tip the scales in favor of elevating men over women. Let's face it: Society has been structured by men and for men.

There have actually been decades of research on this phenomenon of gender disparity in the field of occupational psychology. Research has shown that harassment is more common in historically male-dominated fields, like medicine, fields where big power differentials exist, like medicine, fields where women are in the minority, still like medicine, and especially in certain specialties, and when institutions tolerate the behavior.

Let me be clear: Much of this behavior wasn't necessarily intended to put women down but is rooted in unconscious biases. But what exactly is bias? How many of us actually think we behave in a biased way? Here's a news flash: We are all biased! Bias is how we perceive things—the lenses through which we see the world. It's a cognitive shortcut that shapes our view based on our experiences, our upbringing, and what we've been exposed to. This is why conscious bias is not the same as deliberate discrimination.

Our brains are remarkably designed for one main purpose: survival. Over time, they've evolved to scan the constant influx of information around us, making quick associations that help us make decisions on the fly. Imagine an accountant: They don't show every detail but instead give you the final product that matters. Similarly, our brains process everything we see and hear but filter out anything that doesn't fit our worldview. This "mental accounting" process means we often act on these biases without realizing it, leading to behaviors that continue to reinforce a "lesser-than" status for women in subtle but impactful ways.[21]

In his book *Blink*, Malcolm Gladwell refers to this quick-assessment process as "thin-slicing," where we form gut reactions based on limited, seemingly minor details. These "micropictures" help us navigate decisions efficiently, but they are also influenced by societal norms and expectations ingrained in us from a young age.[22] While useful, this reliance on familiar patterns can make us more susceptible to biases that reflect deeply embedded ideas about gender roles and authority, subtly reinforcing harmful stereotypes even when we don't realize it.

CONSCIOUS AND UNCONSCIOUS BIASES

Historically women were not accepted in most industries. Because they were developed and led by men, most industries continue to be male-dominated. If one went to the Boston Philharmonic back in the 1950s, the majority of constituents in the orchestra were men.[23] In the 1950s approximately only 5 percent of all the symphonies in the United States had women in them. Why was this?

Many presumed it must be because men had an innate ability toward music. Or perhaps, with statistically larger hands, their finger span could stretch further across the strings, thus making a man more facile with an instrument.

In 1952, the Boston Symphony held blind auditions in an attempt to mitigate the gender-related bias that the judges might have had. In this trial, applicants did not speak and played their instruments behind a curtain. The judges were also unaware of their names.

Interestingly there was no change in the percent of women receiving second callback auditions.

During the second phase of the trial, applicants also were told to take off their shoes prior to walking across the stage. After this intervention, the number of women asked to have a second callback increased by 50 percent. Why was this?

Apparently, the clickety-clack of the women's high heels betrayed their sex, and the judges, unconsciously biased against the women, did not select those they heard had noisy shoes. Once applicants removed their shoes, the judges were left to evaluate the applicants as genderless, thus choosing more women.

Sadly for men, they are not innately better at playing instruments than women.

* * *

A similar study was done more recently than 1950 by a technology firm called Speak With a Geek. In this study, performed in 1999, five thousand candidates applied for jobs at technology companies and were presented to a group of employers. The first time around, details like names, experience, and background were provided. Only 5 percent of the applicants selected for further interviews were women.

When identifying details, such as name, were suppressed, that figure jumped to 54 percent. Women asked for a second interview went up from 5 percent to 54 percent by simply eliminating gender-identifying names. The company remarked, "Removing traces of gender or race may prevent employers from basing interview decisions on a conscious or unconscious bias."[24] Conscious bias might manifest as an explicit belief, such as assuming women aren't as adept at coding as men. Unconscious bias, on the other hand, is subtler; for instance, a company might select a male candidate because he aligns more closely with their unexamined image of what a coder "should" look like.

A LOOK INTO POP CULTURE

Examining pop culture, from *Time* magazine covers to Hollywood productions, reveals a landscape deeply marked by gender bias. While high-profile events like the Harvey Weinstein scandals and the #MeToo movement spotlight overt discrimination, more subtle forms of gender inequity continue to pervade entertainment. For instance, gender disparities persist in fields like screenwriting, where women are significantly underrepresented. These biases are even visible in background scenes, where women make up only 17 percent of extras in family-rated films, despite constituting half of the population.[25] Such underrepresentation sends a clear message that women's presence is secondary, even in roles without speaking lines.

Structural biases extend to how female characters are portrayed on screen. Dr. Martha M. Lauzen, a professor of film and television, highlights that gender stereotypes persist in both characterization and visibility.[26] Viewers are often informed of a female character's marital status but rarely of a male character's marital status, while male protagonists are more likely to be depicted physically performing their occupational roles. Additionally, only about one-fourth of all leaders shown on-screen are women. These portrayals reinforce societal expectations about women's roles and contributions, limiting the ways women are represented in popular media. As a result, the biases entrenched in pop culture not only reflect but also perpetuate gender inequality across broader social landscapes, subtly shaping how society views and values women's roles.

Unequal screen time and dialogue further indicate Hollywood's male-centric narrative structures. Research from the Geena Davis Institute reveals that male characters in top-grossing films often receive up to twice as much screen time and dialogue as their female counterparts. Across the top nine hundred films between 2007 and 2016, women held fewer than 31 percent of speaking roles, and in only 12 percent of films were at least half of the characters female.[27] In 2019, just 40 percent of film protagonists were women.

Additionally, most blockbuster movie franchises were made famous and successful by their male leads. Think Harry Potter, *Lord of the Rings*, Star Wars, *The Fast and the Furious*, Pirates of the Caribbean, James Bond, *Jason Bourne*, *Avatar*, and the vast array of movies in the Marvel Cinematic Universe. In comparison, I can think of two comparably big female-led franchises: *The Hunger Games* and *Twilight*.

However, this isn't to say the male-led franchises are staying male-driven, or that the female characters in those stories aren't beloved, or that female-led franchises produce better role models for our daughters. Hermione, Princess Leia, and Elizabeth Swann are some of the most admired characters in film regardless of not being at their story's center. They are loved for their ability to be badasses in a man's world. And as for our protagonists, while Katniss joins this list of powerful women, I can't say that Bella Swan deserves the same praise. (Also please note how all five of these women are played by white actresses. Race inequity and underrepresentation could be another whole book as well.)

Notably, Marvel has been expanding their repertoire in the past years with female-focused stories in *Wonder Woman* (2017) and *Captain Marvel* (2019). However, not all expansions and female shifts have been as seamless. Even in the attempt to introduce a female protagonist, Rey, to the traditionally male-centered Star Wars franchise with *The Force Awakens* (2015), Rey's character was notably downplayed in the film's early marketing campaigns by having less screen time in promotions.[28] Such disparities reveal Hollywood's deep-rooted preference for male-driven stories, which can affect audience perceptions of women's roles in society and reinforce stereotypes about leadership and authority.

These biases also shape children's media, where male characters dominate roles that portray adventure, leadership, and heroism. Disney movies, for example, often position female characters as "princesses" in need of rescue, reinforcing traditional gender roles. More recently, Disney has been focusing on "uncoupled" princesses rather than romance-driven, with characters like Merida from *Brave*, Elsa from *Frozen*, and Moana. Despite this progress, however, the shift toward more independent female characters is still relatively recent, and gender biases continue to influence how children perceive their own potential. When children predominantly see men in action-oriented or leadership roles, it reinforces a belief that boys are inherently more suited to adventure and leadership, while girls are passive or in need of protection. Such representations can have lasting impacts, shaping young girls' self-perception and limiting their aspirations.

Beyond film and television, the scrutiny of female celebrities also reflects a double standard. Stars like Billie Eilish and Taylor Swift have spoken out about how they face greater criticism than their male counterparts, especially regarding their appearance and personal lives. Swift, for instance, has noted that her dating history is frequently highlighted, whereas similar behavior in male celebrities often goes unnoticed.[29] This heightened scrutiny suggests that women's value is tied to their private lives rather than their talents, pressuring them to conform to unrealistic expectations. Such double standards reinforce a culture in which women are disproportionately held accountable for behaviors that are deemed acceptable in men.

A BRIEF LOOK INTO THE POLITICAL ARENA

Medicine, business, pop culture, Hollywood. Now let's take a quick look at politics, an area that determines laws, rights, and regulations that affect our everyday lives and constructs that govern us. For decades, men have benefited from stereotypes around gender in politics, which consistently associate masculinity with effective leadership.[30]

In January 2023, 2,967 women held elected office in the US.[31] This number pales in comparison to the approximately 167.5 million women of all ages in the US.[32] Women make up more than 50 percent of America's population. Yet they hold only 30 percent of elected offices on the federal, state, and local levels—and this 30 percent is a record-breaking high, as more than ever before women are now engaging in political office.[33] A meager 30 percent is impressively low for a "record-breaking high."

Meredith Conroy, a political science professor at California State University, San Bernardino, engaged in a research study to examine the use of gendered language in presidential elections from 2000 to 2012.[34] Examining a random sample of three hundred print-edition news articles from *The New York Times* and *USA Today*, Conroy recorded all traits used to describe all presidential candidates and created what is, in essence, a "traits database." Relying on an existent understanding of "gendered traits" from psychology and political science, traits within the database were labeled as masculine (such as "risk-taker" or "fighter"), feminine (such as "compassionate" or "cautious"), or gender neutral (such as "intelligent," "old" or "liar").[35]

Among the articles examined, 56 percent of the traits recorded as describing presidential candidates were categorized as neutral, 30 percent as masculine, and 14 percent as feminine. The most common masculine traits were "aggressive" and "confident," generally framed in a positive light. The most common feminine traits were "weak" and "inconsistent," generally used negatively. Delving further into the data, Conroy found that, among all feminine traits used to describe candidates, only 31 percent carried a positive tone. Compare this to the overwhelming 67 percent of masculine traits used positively, and it is no surprise that masculinity has become associated with effective political leadership.

Though this study was published in 2015, the use—and potential harm—of gendered language is more relevant now than ever before. And it's no longer as subtle as character traits.

Women in politics also have their clothing choices highly critiqued. Just search "media commentary when Hillary Clinton ran for president," and many articles will pop up. They are composed with critiques on how she looks, how she's aged since being first lady, and her signature pantsuits. One such article found that "any mention of a female candidate's appearance—positive or negative—hurts her chances of being elected into office."[36] I guess you can say progress is being made in that the second time a major US political party nominated a female presidential candidate, Kamala Harris, the news focused less on her wardrobe and appearance. This did not stop the same outcome as before.

✻ ✻ ✻

OK, so why am I talking about Disney princesses, Taylor Swift, and Hillary Clinton's pantsuits? I want to paint a picture of how the stories we tell and the coverage we get as women is inherently biased. I want you to understand that this world is not built for women, that society wants us to aspire to be supporting actresses, love interests, and homemakers, not breadwinners. Movies send messages about what types of roles they want people to play in real life. The news tells us what we should pay attention to and what is important, and politics shapes our reality through laws and showing us what a leader looks like.

So when women are cast as the token supporting female in an action movie, when Taylor Swift is told her worth comes only from writing breakup songs about her latest ex-boyfriend, when female politicians are criticized for their style over their policies, *that* is what society is telling us women are worth. Pretty faces and relationships to men. And God help you if you're not conventionally attractive or whatever society deems is "pretty."

This is the reality in which we live and the society in which I became a doctor. In the coming chapters, I will detail all the ways I learned just how much this was true.

Little did I realize in med school that my future career prospects would not solely be based on my knowledge or budding clinical expertise. I was too young, perhaps too naive, and I was viewing the world with rose-colored glasses. I never realized how gender would impact my future. If we compare two doctors who have the same exact education from the same school, same residency, and same board scores, a male physician will go on to have many more opportunities than a female physician. Opportunities for academic promotion, for research grants, for speaking engagements. They are evaluated more kindly and garner more respect.

No one really shares those details, so I wanted to.

TAKEAWAYS

1. **Systemic gender disparities persist across fields:** From the medical profession to entertainment, gender inequities remain entrenched. These disparities are not merely about pay gaps but extend to opportunities for leadership, recognition, and advancement.
    a. Medicine: Women physicians are less likely to secure tenure, receive NIH funding, or hold leadership roles despite equal credentials.
    b. Entertainment: Women receive less screen time, dialogue, and leading roles, reinforcing societal norms that undervalue their contributions.
2. **Unconscious bias shapes outcomes:** Biases, both conscious and unconscious, continue to hinder women's advancement. These biases manifest in hiring practices, evaluations, and representation in media, perpetuating stereotypes and limiting opportunities.
    a. Examples: The blind auditions for the Boston Symphony Orchestra revealed how removing gender indicators increased women's success rates. Similarly, anonymizing job applications in tech dramatically boosted female candidates' selection rates.
3. **Representation matters:** The underrepresentation of women in leadership roles, on-screen narratives, and panel discussions reinforces harmful stereotypes. Visibility influences societal expectations and shapes how young people perceive their potential.

CHALLENGES TO YOU

1. **Reflect on your biases:** Take some time to write about or discuss the assumptions you might hold—not just about gender but about other aspects of identity like age, race, class, or ability. Consider harmful biases and subtle assumptions that might perpetuate inequality as well as non-harmful or neutral biases that shape your perspective. For instance, when you encounter someone defying traditional expectations or norms (e.g., a young CEO or an older athlete), how do you react? What does that tell you about internalized societal expectations? This reflection can be private or shared with a trusted group to foster dialogue.
2. **Examine the stories you consume:** Consider the books, movies, and TV shows you enjoy. Who are the protagonists? What roles do they occupy? Are there recurring patterns about how different genders or identities are portrayed? How might diversifying your media consumption challenge these perspectives?

Chapter 3

THE PLAYING FIELD IS MALE

"There's nothing a man can do that I can't do better and in heels."
—WIDELY ATTRIBUTED TO GINGER ROGERS

I entered Columbia University College of Physicians and Surgeons in the fall of 1990. I was one of 120 or so. Certainly, the proportion of males to females was uneven, with more men than women, both as students and as teachers. Medicine was a male domain.

This carried through to my internship, anesthesia residency, and critical care fellowship, where I was the only woman of five critical care fellows in the postsurgical intensive care units. Most attendings I learned from were male. The chair of the department of anesthesia was male. The chief of the critical care service line was male. The didactic weekly sessions were run by a man. Most surgeons I interacted with regarding their ICU patients were male. I must admit, this did not seem unusual to me. Even by this point, early in my career, I'd come to expect men to be in charge.

This carried over into my first job as well. After fellowship, I decided to move north and took a job at a large public hospital in New England. This was it. I'd finally made it! I was starting my first "real" job, not in training anymore. I looked forward to growing my expertise and skills alongside colleagues who were equally passionate about what they did. I found this job because a friend and co-resident who was a few years ahead of me had joined this group and really liked it. It had the full scope of anesthesia cases: thoracic, cardiac, peds, trauma, obstetrics, and general cases as well as an attending presence in the intensive care units that I could join. It also had the opportunity to teach residents in anesthesia and medical students from two schools; it was a blend of private practice and academia. The best of both worlds!

I started out in August of 1999 and was hired to start on the same day as three male colleagues. That turned out to be about the same proportion, 25 percent, of women in the group at the time. Although the number of doctors in the practice has grown over the twenty-four years I've practiced there, having approximately quadrupled in size, the proportion of female to male attendings remains about the same. Over my years, there has never been a female chair of the department of anesthesia, or head of the anesthesia residency, or assistant residency director. Eighty percent of the years, the managing director of our division, the private practice component, has been male. The year a woman took over, she was the only person on the ballot.

Why do I mention this?

It has become apparent that this illustrates male privilege, a culture built by men for men.

If men are the leaders, they are in control. They are the gatekeepers who determine who will receive resources, which, in my sphere, often is nonclinical time. They allocate time off clinical duty to pursue scholarly pursuits. This leads to the production of research, which leads to promotions, especially in the academic realm, which leads to professorships, which leads to more money and prestige. The male leaders also determine who will be on committees, often choosing just one woman to be the "token" female. I found myself exactly in this position when I was asked to be part of the residency interviewing team. This is the team that interviews the medical students who are applying to our program for residency and who have passed the first set of screening and been invited for interviews.

During the course of the interview day, the medical students receive a tour from a male colleague of mine and then sit down to interview with the chair, the residency director, the co-director, the ex-chair, and me. All those other positions were held by men, so they wanted a woman. When they approached me and asked if I would join the committee, they literally said, "Well, we need a woman. You can be the 'token female,'" and they chuckled. I, of course, rolled with it, too eager to be included in the inner circle. I suppose I was just grateful they chose me, never really processing their comments.

* * *

The group I joined was a private practice group, for profit, which was focused on revenue generation. Don't get me wrong; they wanted us to give good care, but unless you were in the operating room performing anesthetics, you were a negative on the balance sheet. There was no time for leadership development. No time for courses. No time for research. Our hospital had not yet fully embraced its academic standing, and certainly, our group did not support non-lucrative endeavors. There also was no formal mentorship structure and no guidance related to career development. No one asked, "Where do you want to see yourself, in your career, in five or ten years?"

There also were very few female role models to look up to. Again, my group, the surgeons, and the hospital leadership positions were very male-dominated. In my organization, the leadership teams, such as chairs, department heads, and residency directors, and the governing boards, including my group's private practice CEO, CFO, and board members, were almost exclusively male. All around me, control was in male hands. One or two more senior women would pass down some pearls, like "Don't ever get rid of call because you'll be the last to leave every day." But beyond an occasional piece of advice, no mentoring happened.

The people in places I aspired to were not like me. They were men. I found often that men seemed to "buddy up" to other men. Of course, people like to help younger versions of themselves, and so often male leaders mentor other young men. It is not accidental that more men than women have mentors in medicine.

MALE-DOMINATED SPACES

In the UK, a study of children aged seven through eleven asked them to draw and name a person who performs certain jobs—a banker, a builder, and a nurse. The results were telling: 81 percent of children drew nurses as female, while 88 percent drew builders as male and 80 percent drew bankers as male.[37] These early assumptions about who "should" do certain jobs highlight the unconscious biases that persist into adulthood.

Male-dominated work spheres often have men in charge, reinforcing the belief that leadership belongs to men. When this is combined with preconceived notions about which gender "should" perform certain roles, women in leadership positions are frequently misunderstood or overlooked. For example, in a male-dominated field like medicine, many still assume the attending physician—a role traditionally seen as male—is a man. This presumption persists even when the female attending has clearly established her leadership.

I experienced this firsthand during an interaction in the ICU a few years ago. As the attending physician, I led a large team that day: three residents (one from anesthesia, one surgical resident, and one from emergency medicine), an advanced practice provider, a pharmacist, and several medical students. During one round, I entered a patient's room accompanied by a male medical student who looked to be Doogie Howser incarnate (an old '90s television reference; for those of you unfamiliar, Doogie Howser was the star of a sitcom by the same name, played by a young Neil Patrick Harris. He was a prodigy who graduated medical school at the age of fourteen). I, on the other hand, had gray hair at my temples, despite my attempts to color over it, and enough wrinkles to consume all the Botox on the eastern seaboard. There was no way our age difference was not apparent.

When I began to relay to the family of this sick patient what clinically was happening to their loved one, they stopped me mid-sentence. They wanted only Doogie to speak.

"Sorry, honey, but we want to hear it from the doctor." They motioned for my med student to take over.

This is an example of role incredulity—a phenomenon in

which people doubt a woman's ability to hold a position of authority. It's a reality many women face. I've seen female surgeons carefully explain preoperative plans to patients, only to be asked afterward, "When will I get a chance to talk to the surgeon?" The patient is unable to fathom that the woman before them *is* the surgeon.

A classic riddle illustrates this same bias: A teenage boy and his father are in a car accident and rushed to the ER. The attending surgeon looks at the boy and says, "I can't operate on this boy. He's my son!" How can this be? Five decades after the riddle first appeared, many people still fail to answer it correctly: The surgeon is the boy's mother.

This mindset, which makes the answer to the riddle elusive, continues to permeate medical spaces, casting doubt on women's authority. For female physicians, the need to constantly reintroduce themselves as the attending, the physician in charge, or the board-certified expert is exhausting and demoralizing. When families or patients hold these ingrained beliefs, it often manifests as doubts about the female physician's competence. If a physician expresses frustration in response, she risks receiving a negative review or a formal complaint. Such outcomes can harm evaluations, damage reputations, and impede career advancement. The emotional toll of these dynamics is immense and deeply unfair.

Failure to recognize the authority of women may be the purview of not just the patients and their families. Even when women are in leadership roles, some men working below them may not wish to recognize their roles and they may thus work around them.

At one point in my career, I was elected to a position intimately related to scheduling all our staff—allocating staff in off-site locations, main operating rooms, and ambulatory surgical centers. Because I needed to know when there were increased or decreased demands in staffing, when the hospital was providing holidays, when staff would be out for personal reasons, etc., I was in a position that needed to know things. I was often excluded from meetings where these types of issues were discussed. I then would find out days later, sometimes by accidentally overhearing conversations, that I needed to adjust staffing. This made my job harder, less efficient, more stressful, and, frankly, very frustrating. Eventually, it led me to speak to my chair and discuss my concerns and frustrations. I told him I would be stepping down from my position if I wasn't included in those meetings.

Another one of my female colleagues was facing a similar situation. She was directly in charge of overseeing all the residency programs at our institution in a position titled the designated institutional officer, or DIO. It's a huge job with lots of responsibility. Our departmental chair never seemed to report our residency issues to her but instead went to her male superior. She asked him politely to stop doing this and to directly involve her in communications. He never did. He continuously sidestepped her, making her job harder and overtly disrespecting her and her position. He was never admonished by the institution. The culture, from the top down, seemed to condone this.

※ ※ ※

Unfortunately, if you are male, you may not see or feel any of these issues. You are lucky that the system was created for you by a person who most likely looks like you. That is the basis of white male privilege.

Some women, too, are blindly unaware of how gender impacts women's experiences. They personally have not perceived discrimination and thus discount its very existence. Some may even have benefited from a certain leader's actions—by receiving a promotion, for example—and therefore cannot believe that the same person is setting limitations on other women or is promoting a male-dominated culture. Often it is easier to look the other way or not see uncomfortable truths. An extreme yet poignant example is that a man who sexually assaults one woman does not need to sexually assault all women to be a rapist. Let that sink in.

TAKEAWAYS

1. **The impact of systemic privilege is real:** Male-dominated systems often perpetuate themselves by design, granting more opportunities, resources, and mentorship to men. When leadership and decision-making are concentrated in male hands, it creates cycles of exclusion that are difficult for women to break. Recognizing these dynamics is the first step toward dismantling them.
2. **Role incredulity is real and harmful:** Women in positions of authority frequently encounter skepticism about their competence or legitimacy, even when they've earned their roles. This doubt, whether from patients, colleagues, or supervisors, has tangible consequences, creating additional hurdles for women in male-dominated spaces.
3. **Mentorship shapes careers:** The lack of mentorship and guidance for women often limits their professional growth. Male leaders, consciously or unconsciously, usually mentor other men, leaving women to navigate their careers without the same support systems. Proactive efforts to mentor women are essential to countering these disparities.
4. **Unseen biases reinforce stereotypes:** Early gender-based assumptions about who "should" perform certain roles are reinforced by society, media, and professional environments. These biases must be actively challenged to create a more inclusive workplace where leadership isn't tied to gender.

CHALLENGES TO YOU

1. Recognize and challenge role incredulity in medicine.
   a. Pay attention to interactions where a female physician's expertise is doubted. Have you ever witnessed a patient assume a male medical student or resident was the attending over a female attending?
   b. If you experience or observe role incredulity, consider how you can correct the assumption, whether by reinforcing a female colleague's authority in front of patients or speaking up when women's leadership is ignored in meetings.
   c. The next time you introduce yourself to a new patient, be mindful of how they respond. Do they seem surprised? Skeptical? Track these interactions over a month, and reflect on any patterns.
2. Challenge the "default male" mindset in medicine.
   a. Test your own unconscious biases by reflecting on how you perceive leadership. Do you instinctively associate authority in medicine with men?
   b. If you are responsible for hiring, promotions, or academic opportunities, actively ensure a diverse applicant pool, and evaluate whether gender plays an unconscious role in selection.
   c. If you're a male colleague, make space for women to lead, whether by deferring speaking time in meetings, acknowledging women's expertise in front of patients, or ensuring female colleagues receive credit for their work.

Chapter 4

A NAME IS JUST A NAME, OR IS IT?

"A name is the first and most important thing we give to a person, and it is a marker of identity. It is a foundation for every relationship."

—BRYAN STEVENSON[38]

Throughout my medical school training, internship, residency, and attendingship, I have been addressed as many things: Blondilocks, Miss, Honey, Blondie, Nurse, hey you, baby, Kolleen. After years of hard work, sleepless nights, and endless exams, I graduated from medical school. A huge accomplishment and a life dream. I am a bona fide, card-carrying "doctor." However, I was still called these other things. This didn't seem to happen to my male colleagues. They were always called "Doctor."

At first, it was subtle. I was just getting used to my new title. I would shrug it off and not read into it. If I asked others, they would tell me to not take it too seriously. Who cared? I tried to tell myself I didn't need the external validation. I knew I was a doctor, so did it really matter? I also began to wonder if I was somehow inadvertently sending off some informal vibe that signaled that I preferred that colleagues and patients called me by my first name. But when I chatted with my female physician friends, I realized it was *not* just me. Every female doctor had the experience of being called by her first name. It was ubiquitous.

Whether it was by a patient, by a family member, in the operating room, at a lecture hall, or in an office, we were called by our first names or a generic female call.

My femaleness somehow invited familiarity.

I have been in the presence of male colleagues, who all are addressed by their title, Dr. So-and-So, while I am, in the same sentence, addressed as simply Kolleen. Don't get me wrong; sometimes a first name is fine, but why the dichotomy? Why are men Doctor and I'm just my first name?

A study in 2017 from ASU and the Mayo Clinic found that when men introduced female speakers, they were statistically significantly more likely to introduce the woman by her first name rather than her title compared to when they introduced a male speaker.[39]

Choice of words matters and can have ramifications that go beyond mere ego.

Those ramifications can include roadblocks to professional development, being perceived as having less authority, and being taken less seriously in one's profession. It gets down to the perception of expertise and the perception of competence. Failure to acknowledge a woman's hard-earned professional title while men are awarded theirs, even when unintentional, has profound implications and reinforces the perception of women having lower status. This "deprofessionalizing" serves to activate stereotype threat and internalized sexism at a time when a woman needs to be at peak performance, whether she's speaking, teaching, or caring for her patients.

* * *

This phenomenon occurs frequently in male-dominated industries like politics, where power dynamics play a significant role. During the 2016 US presidential election, Hillary Clinton made history as the first female candidate nominated by a major political party. Regardless of political affiliation, her candidacy was a monumental step forward for women. However, Clinton was often referred to by her first name, "Hillary," while her male counterparts, like "Biden" and "Trump," were typically referred to by their last names.[40] While some argue that this was done to differentiate her from her husband, former president Bill Clinton, it highlights a larger issue in how women are addressed in public life.

Interestingly, this pattern persisted during the 2024 US presidential election when Kamala Harris became the second woman nominated by a major political party. Kamala Harris was often referred to as Kamala, and Donald Trump was referred to as Trump, not Donald. I will await the actual analysis and data extraction on this one, but I imagine it will share the same trends as before. This informal address reflects a broader issue in gender dynamics.

Deborah Tannen, a linguistics professor at Georgetown University, explains that even when using a first name is intended to signal friendliness, it often results in the person being shown less respect.[41] This is particularly true for women in positions of power, as it undermines their authority. Similarly, Laura F. Edwards, a history professor who focuses on gender studies at Duke University, notes that calling women by their first names ties into historical traditions where women took their fathers' or husbands' last names because they weren't expected to have public roles.[42] This practice persists today in how women are acknowledged—or diminished—in professional spheres.

These subtle linguistic choices reflect a larger societal problem that continues to undermine women's authority in male-dominated fields like politics, medicine, and corporate leadership. This tendency to refer to women by their first names, whether intentional or not, reflects a deeper issue of gender bias in professional settings. While it may seem like a small detail, it serves to subtly undermine their authority, particularly in male-dominated industries like politics and medicine. This linguistic diminishment echoes the broader, more personal experiences of many women in these fields—where their qualifications and expertise are often disregarded or overshadowed by their male counterparts. And it extends beyond just first-naming women.

* * *

I had no idea that disregarding my accomplishments and the title I worked so hard for was part of something called "tall poppy syndrome."

But there it was, a term for this phenomenon I was experiencing in an article I came across. The term tall poppy syndrome originated in Australia and New Zealand, where it's so common they even teach it in schools.[43] Poppies grow tall, and those that grow taller than others are sometimes not allowed to thrive—in these countries, while people are happy to see you succeed, if you stand out too much, they'll cut you down to size.[44] Essentially, it describes how successful people can be disliked or criticized just because they're successful.

Now let's apply tall poppy syndrome in the hospital. While

the original phrase doesn't necessarily have to do with gender, I thought about how much it applies to female physicians—like in the example above, how my hard-earned doctor title was often bypassed to my first name, or even a diminutive nickname, by patients and colleagues alike. I didn't realize that the act of undermining a woman's achievements, diminishing her success, or resenting her had a specific name.

Let's take an even bigger step out to include women in the workforce worldwide. A study by Dr. Rumeet Billan in 2023 looked at over 4,700 respondents across more than 100 countries. She found that 86.8 percent of women are penalized at work because of their achievements.[45] Women reported that 77 percent had their achievements downplayed, 73 percent had their achievements ignored or left out of acknowledgments completely, and 66 percent had their successes credited to others.[46] Certainly, over time, this can contribute to a woman feeling undervalued.

Women pull other women down; those in peer or colleague positions most frequently cut down other women, likely in an attempt to step over them and get ahead. But Dr. Billan's research also revealed that this behavior isn't exclusive to women—everyone does it, with position and title playing a key role. Men in senior leadership often undermine women.

Names matter. Perhaps mine should now be Poppy.

TAKEAWAYS

1. **Names and titles carry power:** Names and titles carry significant weight and reflect identity, authority, and the way society perceives and respects us. Consistently addressing someone by their professional title reinforces their expertise and credibility, particularly in male-dominated fields where women often face systemic bias.
2. **Deprofessionalization plays a role in undermining authority:** Subtle linguistic choices, such as addressing women by their first names while referring to men by their titles, may seem trivial but can have profound impacts. This practice diminishes women's authority, affects their professional development, and perpetuates perceptions of incompetence.
3. **Tall poppy syndrome undermines achievement:** The phenomenon of cutting down those who stand out—whether due to success, expertise, or ambition—disproportionately affects women in the workplace, from downplaying accomplishments to outright disregarding them. This behavior reinforces a culture of devaluation and impedes the progression of women in leadership roles.

CHALLENGES TO YOU

1. **Audit address practices:** Reflect on how you address and introduce professionals in your workplace. Do you instinctively call women by their first names while using titles for men? Make a conscious effort to use professional titles consistently for all colleagues, especially in formal settings. For example:
   a. Instead of: "Here's Emily and Dr. Smith."
   b. Say: "Here's Dr. Parker and Dr. Smith."
2. **Set clear expectations:** As a professional, take the initiative to introduce yourself how you want to be addressed. While some situations may call for a more casual atmosphere, first names should never automatically be the default—especially for women who have worked hard to earn their medical degree. Using your professional title can help reinforce your role as the expert in the room and build trust with patients and their families. If someone misaddresses you, correct them gently but confidently while maintaining a collaborative tone. For example: "Thank you for your question. Before we proceed, I'd like to clarify that I prefer to be called Dr. Parker, as it helps distinguish my role and acknowledges my qualifications." This approach not only communicates your preferences but also fosters awareness about the importance of equitable and respectful forms of address in professional settings.
3. **Address tall poppy syndrome:** If you notice achievements being downplayed or ignored, speak up. Acknowledge and celebrate the successes of your colleagues, especially women, to counteract the culture of devaluation. For example: "I noticed that Dr. Jackson's contribution wasn't mentioned earlier. It played a key role in the success of this project."

Chapter 5

PERKY AS A JOB REQUIREMENT (IF FEMALE)

"If I hear the word 'perky' again, I'll puke."
—KATIE COURIC[47]

The societal norm for women is to be "nurturing," the "caregiver," and more emotionally connected. Women often shoulder the tasks that are emotionally based, such as chairing the social committee and being the person to host baby showers, retirement parties, and group holiday events. Women often are asked to do these things or often it is just expected. In my group, for my entire twenty-four years, only women have hosted the social committee. One woman has brought in brownies or cookies every Wednesday for twenty-plus years! I have heard many say, "What are we going to do when she retires? Who will bring the brownies?" This demeans her role as a caring physician, and instead of focusing on her professional accomplishments, overseeing one of our subspecialty areas in the anesthesia department, it focuses on her Betty Crocker skills.

Sociologist Dr. Arlie Hochschild coined the term "emotional labor."[38] She describes it as "putting another's feelings and desires before your own." Often expected in the service industry, emotional labor is about displaying certain emotions when interacting with colleagues or, in this case, patients, as well as managing their emotional responses. For example, waiters are expected to be accommodating and polite, teachers to show encouragement and enthusiasm, and doctors to stay calm under pressure. However, female workers, across all professions, also carry the extra expectation to be cheery. My chair used the term "perky."

I will admit I try to be upbeat and happy all the time. I try to manage my thoughts and feelings to look at the bright side and not let negativity affect me. But it can be hard when you do not feel valued at an organization.

In the fall of 2019, our chair decided to revamp our anesthesia offices. There were many people now in the group, and the number of staff far outgrew the number of available office spaces. He decided to allocate space per subspecialty and have most everyone pick up and move. Not an easy task when one has been in the same office for over fifteen years. But we all did it—well, not exactly all. Many did it, including me. I had to pack everything up—my files, books, pictures—and move across the hall to what was going to be the shared ICU office. However, all the desks in the ICU office were already occupied by ICU staff, leaving no space for me. My husband came in one night, after hours, and helped me box everything up. Fifteen-plus years of notes and files all in a box moved to my home basement.

Others simply did not move. They ignored the chair's directive and, to my surprise, had no ill consequence for this. Why did I listen, if it was optional? Why am I always a rule follower?

Not only did I take my personal time and my husband's time to move everything, but I no longer felt like I had a place to sit between cases, to store my stuff. I could not have at my fingertips the books and articles I had accumulated in my career. I also felt undervalued. It's hard to feel valued when you aren't even given a place to sit down.

* * *

One day I was called into my chair's office, summoned there by a page. I felt overwhelmed. Never had I been called to the chair's office for a meeting. I had no idea what was wrong. I was nervous. Did I do something wrong? It felt like being called to the principal's office, something that was completely foreign to me, as I'd never had that happen before in my entire life.

He asked quite blankly, "Why are you not perky?"

I was taken aback. "Excuse me?" I asked.

"I noticed that you are not as perky as usual, and I'd like you to be more perky."

"I'm sorry, but am I not performing at my job?"

"No, no, you are great. Everyone loves you. You do a great job."

"Well, why am I being summoned here?"

"You just don't seem perky."

"I didn't realize that was part of my job requirement. Are you calling all the men who have groused around the department for the last twenty years here to discuss their perkiness?"

"No."

Then silence.

I don't think he liked my calling out his double standard on work expectations or the extra emotional labor expected of women at work but not of men.

I felt like from that point on, we were on a course bound to crash.

※ ※ ※

Women, along with having to be "perky," often are saddled with the "office housework," or non-promotable tasks. These tasks might include serving on low-level committees, organizing holiday soirees, reorganizing the resident library, or tasks that do not require much skill or provide much impact. All these tasks might need to be done but certainly will not make commentary on one's performance review or lead to career advancements. The "housework" might be assigned to the women staff or, sadly, women themselves often volunteer for it.

Research published in *Harvard Business Review* indicates that women in mixed-gender groups were asked to volunteer 44 percent more often than men. Notably, the manager's gender had no impact—both male and female managers were more likely to approach women for such tasks. This choice seemed strategic, as women were more inclined to agree; men accepted 51 percent of volunteer requests, while women said yes 76 percent of the time.[49]

TAKEAWAYS

1. **Women are held to different emotional standards than men:** In the workplace, women are expected to exhibit traits like perkiness, warmth, and cheerfulness—qualities rarely demanded of their male counterparts. These expectations add an invisible layer of pressure to maintain emotional composure, often at the expense of being taken seriously or valued for their professional expertise.
2. **Emotional labor disproportionately falls on women:** Tasks like planning social events, baking for the office, or managing interpersonal dynamics are frequently assigned to or expected of women. While these contributions create a positive environment, they are rarely acknowledged as part of one's professional achievements. Instead, they overshadow significant accomplishments and reinforce gendered expectations.
3. **"Office housework" stalls women's careers:** Women are often asked to perform—or volunteer for—tasks like organizing low-level committees, managing shared spaces, or hosting office events. These duties, though important, do not contribute to career advancement or performance reviews. This unpaid labor adds to women's workloads without the corresponding professional benefits.

CHALLENGES TO YOU

Evaluate your own workload: Are you spending a significant amount of time on emotional labor or non-promotable tasks? If so:

1. **Set boundaries:** Politely decline tasks that don't align with your goals or job responsibilities.
2. **Prioritize impactful work:** Focus your efforts on assignments that contribute to your career growth or enhance your skills.
3. **Advocate for fair distribution:** Encourage balanced task delegation to ensure everyone shares in the responsibilities of the workplace.

Chapter 6

THE TIGHTROPE, OR THE LIKABILITY CONUNDRUM

"If you just set out to be liked, you would be prepared to compromise on anything at any time and you would achieve nothing."
—MARGARET THATCHER[50]

I was talking with one of the female anesthesia residents who I had spent the day teaching in the ICU. I asked if she ever felt she was treated differently because of her gender. She said that she did not but then went on to tell me that as long as she spoke extra nice and made chitchat with the other staff in the ICU or operating room, they liked her. She recounted that another one of her female co-residents wasn't having as easy a time because the other resident typically was all business. I followed up with another question.

"Do you think the male residents do that, make chitchat before getting down to business, in order to be liked before performing their job duties?"

There was silence.

How many of us have noticed that being a female doctor is much harder? You have to be authoritative in a code but not overbearing. Command the situation but not be too controlling. You have to be liked or you come across as b*tchy. You are either too loud or not assertive, too quiet and then not willing to take charge when needed. Your concerns are seen as whining while a male counterpart is seen as having legitimate issues, even if they're the same. Formally, this phenomenon is called the "double bind."[51] Informally, I think of it as a tightrope.

The fact is, although women make up over 50 percent of the average medical school classes right now, in society's eyes, we are still supposed to be more demure, more accommodating.[52] Just like we have this unwritten expectation to be perky, we are socialized to be nurturing, submissive, and supportive. If we exhibit agentic traits, which are typically male traits—assertive, confident, loud—it creates cognitive dissonance and is met with disapproval.

Let's take a closer look at adjectives used to describe men versus women in the workplace. The desire for leadership roles to embody traits like assertiveness, decisiveness, competitiveness, and confidence is often called the "male blueprint," as these characteristics are traditionally associated with masculinity.[53] When looking at the characteristics in job descriptions associated with men, there's an emphasis on assertiveness and leadership; words like "competitive," "dominant," "determined," "independent," and "driven" are more often used in job postings for positions typically occupied by men or in male-dominated fields.[54] This includes doctors. There's also a focus on technical expertise; roles tend to emphasize specific technical skills or competencies, with less focus on soft skills or emotional intelligence. On the other hand, when looking at characteristics associated with women, there's more of an emphasis on collaboration and support: words like "supportive," "nurturing," "empathetic," "team-oriented," and "collaborative."[55] This goes back to women playing the supporting roles on the (male) lead's stage. There's also an emphasis on flexibility and multitasking associated with women since these traits lend themselves to traditionally feminine domains like caregiving or administration.

Men are also more often hired even if they have less experience on their résumés than their female counterparts. In 2014, *Harvard Business Review* released a statistic that said men applied for jobs that they were 60 percent qualified for in terms of past experiences or hard skills, whereas women waited for that 100 percent.[56] This is because men are hired for their perceived future potential, whereas women are hired for their past accomplishments. As a result, men are able to secure prestigious positions at a younger age, while women must first demonstrate proven competence to be considered for similar roles.

The schism of gendered language persists in letters of recommendation as well. Though men may have less experience listed on their résumés, their letters of recommendation often stand out with concrete achievements and statistics. In contrast, women's letters tend to focus more on personality and effort rather than skills or leadership potential. For a man, a letter might highlight his agency using words that emphasize assertiveness, independence, and leadership. Common descriptors include "leader," "driven," "ambitious," "innovative," and "strong."[57] The letter highlights his skills and accomplishments and describes his potential to grow and readiness to lead. It highlights his professionalism and measurable impact with phrases like "outstanding contributions" or "high potential for future success."

Now, let's compare these descriptors with how a woman's letter of recommendation might look. Again, there's this emphasis on communality, how much of a "team player" she is. The letter highlights her efforts over her skills or natural abilities with words like "hard-working," "dedicated," or "conscientious."[58] This can downplay the woman's inherent talents or capabilities. And lastly, there's an emphasis on her likability or personality rather than her professionalism—descriptions might include "friendly," "supportive," or "kind"—while downplaying leadership or assertiveness.

All these instances—job descriptions, résumés, letters of recommendation—reek of gender bias. These trends reinforce traditional gender stereotypes in the workplace, which can affect hiring and promotion decisions. Women are often seen as less authoritative and more communal, while men are associated with leadership and innovation, potentially disadvantaging women in competitive roles.

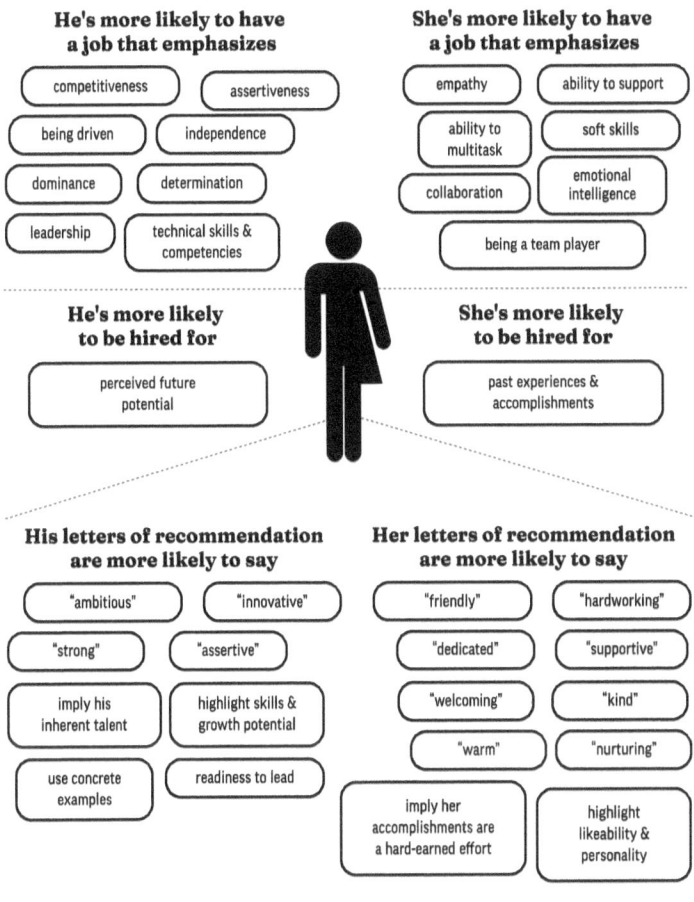

* * *

After learning this, I reflected on how I typically write my evaluations of female residents in comparison to how I write evaluations of male residents. I realized I do it too! We all do it.

I use more "female" adjectives for the women and "masculine" terms for the men. This is a problem because most of what are seen as "male traits" are those employers look for when hiring and advancing.

I now choose words more carefully.

I take opportunities to educate about gender bias and how pervasive and unconscious it is. Little things like committees termed "manpower" need to change to "peoplepower."

The tightrope walk has to stop. Women are balancing over the precipice daily, and it is slowly killing their joy and passion for the careers they spent their lives training for, so they either walk away or, worse yet, fall off the tightrope altogether.

The tightrope I refer to is the one any working woman in medicine or any professional field knows. You know, the one where you have to be nice or you're labeled a b*tch. You see female surgeons doing it daily in the operating room, making small talk prior to a big case so when they need to ask for a different instrument than the one that was pulled, they can get it without seeming "needy" or "difficult to work with." Or on the medical wards where inquiry about the patient's urine output is preceded by "Sorry to bother you, but…" Trying to wield authority when needed during codes but not be shrieky or overbearing. Attempting to be decisive, authoritarian, but not dictatorial.

Studies have shown that women are viewed much more harshly than men when running a code even when scripted narratives are the same. Women are "supposed" to be nurturing and caring, *not* commanding and decisive. Agentic traits typically sociologically reserved for men are met with a cognitive dissonance if present in women. It goes against the cultural norm, the expected, and thus is consciously or many times subconsciously met with disapproval. Ah, the tightrope. Wow. My head spins just thinking of it.

* * *

The good news, kind of, for female doctors is we are not alone. Female college professors are graded more harshly than their male peers even if tests are returned on the same day and the material taught is exactly the same. Men are "supposed" to be the smartest ones, the esteemed professors.[59] Recently, Hamilton College introduced some initiatives to attempt to decrease the stereotypical gender bias in professor evaluations. Despite their attempts, gender-biased evals persisted, showcasing just how ingrained these biases are. This obviously can impact hiring, tenure, promotion, and salary decisions.

Women also are passed up for promotion more than male peers because of the "baby tax," expected time off for child-rearing, which they may or may not ever take.[60] They are less likely to receive NIH funding.[61] They are less likely to be asked to be on a panel; ergo, the term for many all-male conference panels is "manel."[62] Women are less likely to be promoted to chair, less likely to receive mentorship, and thus less likely to stay in their careers. Can we blame them? No, but we often do.

Women are told to "lean in." We tell them to stop sitting in the periphery but to take a seat at the table. We tell them to do yoga, meditate, and find the elusive work-life balance, which may be harder to find than the fountain of eternal youth.

I have an idea.

How about we stop blaming the victims, the women, and create work cultures in which women are not seen as second to men? Create a culture in which women are at the table and given the time to talk, without interruption. We need to create transparent evaluation tools and promotion platforms. We need to educate everyone about unconscious bias and how behavior befitting a man is also befitting a woman and vice versa.

We need equal visibility in leadership roles and panels. Equal opportunity to thrive.

We need consequences for those who perpetuate a culture of inequality. Those who perpetuate the concept that women are not rising to leadership roles because they take time off to have children. We need consequences for those who choose to reinforce biases based on how women "should" behave, and we should not retaliate against those who do challenge the cultural normative female and male stereotypes. Institutions need to lead by example and have more inclusive boards and C-suite executives. Representation matters. Mentorship matters.

Studies have shown that men are more likely to be mentored by senior hospital leaders than females.[63] This harkens back to the famous Heidi versus Howard Harvard Business School case study. Participants in the study were handed one of two applications, either for Heidi or for Howard. The catch was these applications were identical in terms of qualifications and experience; the only difference was the name. While both were equally capable, Howard was described as more likable and more of a leader while Heidi was described as "too aggressive."[64]

Women leaders walk a tightrope. If you lack confidence, you likely won't succeed. If you display as much confidence as many men, you likely won't succeed. I think awareness in the workplace is helping, but there are still wide gaps in expectations for acceptable behavior for women. Recent research shows that male scientists are much more flowery in praise for their own work, reporting in published papers that the findings are "unprecedented, remarkable."[65] Women are more factual and blander in self-description, and those differences may finally impact pay and promotion. The fine line between doormat and b*tch is tough to walk, and I think the difficulty of that tightrope act is a major reason we aren't close to gender parity at senior levels.

TAKEAWAYS

1. **Beware of the double bind or the tightrope:** Women are expected to lead without being "bossy," command respect without losing likability, and succeed without threatening the status quo—an exhausting balancing act that penalizes them no matter how they proceed.
2. **Systemic change starts with personal accountability:** Cultural change is enforced through systemic shifts, but it begins at the individual level. Reflect on how your word choices, actions, and assumptions might unknowingly reinforce biases, even if you belong to a marginalized group yourself.
3. **Representation and mentorship matter:** Equitable workplaces require proactive representation in leadership roles, transparent evaluation systems, and meaningful mentorship opportunities that help women and minorities thrive at every stage of their careers.

CHALLENGES TO YOU

1. **Rethink gendered evaluations:** When you evaluate colleagues, ask yourself, "Do I rely on stereotypical language? Do I use agentic traits for men while assigning communal traits to women?" Adjust your language to reflect individuals' skills and accomplishments equitably.
2. **Reframe your thinking:** Consider how you describe strengths across genders. A male mentee who nurtures others' potential is demonstrating emotional intelligence, a key leadership trait. A female mentee who delegates effectively shows decisive leadership. Use specific examples to highlight their abilities in ways that challenge conventional biases.
3. **Advocate for change:** Beyond personal reflection, advocate for systemic improvements—transparent promotion practices, unconscious bias training, and mentorship programs that uplift diverse talent. It's not enough to change your perspective; help create environments where others can thrive too.

Chapter 7

THE MOTHERHOOD TAX

"*We expect women to work like they don't have children and raise children as if they don't work.*"

—EVE RODSKY[66]

Where to begin?

Should it be the cow doll that my partner at work gave me after my first child was born because I was lactating? Or the fact that my male colleagues repeatedly snarked that I masterminded all four of my children to be born in the summer so I could get summers "off"? Just to clarify, my first two children were born in January and October—certainly not summer in New England. Secondly, any woman knows that having a newborn, exclusively breastfeeding for the first months, enduring endless sleepless nights, all while caring for other children is no summer vacation (I had four children in five and a half years). I'll be honest: Most times I felt like giving anesthesia or running an intensive care unit was easier than packing four tired, cranky children into a car and going to Target to buy three boxes of different-sized diapers.

Motherhood has been the source of my greatest joy. I am a proud mom of two girls and two boys.

For many men and women, having children is a life goal. Becoming a parent and experiencing the highs and lows of raising a little one is a wondrous thing. It is not only wondrous for you and your partner but also for the human race; without people choosing to become parents, the race would become extinct. Our very essence depends on succession. However, when facing a pregnancy, often just as a woman is launching her career, she is filled with mixed emotions. Joy, nervousness, and fear in telling their good news to their workmates. Fear because often if you go out on maternity leave, it means your workload just shifts to your peers. As much as they might like you, they often do not want to take three months' worth of your call because you decided to have your bundle of joy.

I approached my managing partner, ready to tell him of my pregnancy and desire to take a twelve-week maternity leave, with nervous excitement. At that point, I had been at my group for only a little over a year. Not yet a partner, I feared that this might delay me in attaining partnership. I feared how my leave would impact others' call schedules and daily tasks. I feared that they might see me as someone less than 100 percent dedicated to my job.

I entered his office, took a deep breath, and just decided to tell him straight away, "I have some exciting news. Chris [my husband] and I are expecting a baby." Without a moment's pause, he retorted, "Congratulations. But I already knew." Shocked, having told no one, not even our families yet, never mind anyone at work, I wondered how he could have known. The question must have registered on my face because he quickly added, "I knew because your boobs have changed sizes."

I was flabbergasted. Did I just hear him correctly? My boob size?

It's not as though I wear clothes that are tight across my chest. I'm in bland, nondescript, oversized scrubs, for goodness' sake—the most unflattering apparel ever! (This was all before Figs, Jaanuu Scrubs, and GreenCloud.) Certainly not form-fitting. How could he have noticed this? Was he staring more intently than I ever realized? And even if he did unbelievably notice, did he really just say that? I am no legal scholar, but even I knew this could not be considered appropriate commentary from my supervising partner.

I left his office, honestly with mixed emotions of shock at his comments yet relief that I told him. I never reported his comments to anyone other than my husband. I was certainly not going to make a complaint. He was my boss, the most senior man in the group that I wanted to be a partner in. I was just relieved that he did not mention a partnership vote delay, and thus I felt a little indebted to him. How could I, an underling, a mere non-partner associate, lodge a complaint? Certainly, if I wanted to make a partner, it was clear I had to ignore his comments, shove them down, and move on. And so I did, this time and the many other times when off-color comments were made about me or other women. I was conditioned to let it slide and roll off my back.

Every working woman knows the challenges faced when returning to work. There are all the emotional hurdles: the dread of missing a "first" that your precious newborn does, a first smile or first word, the concern that your child will fall in love with whoever is caring for them while you are "missing" at work, the feeling of abandoning your child when they need you most. Ah, the mother's guilt.

But there also are the physical challenges. You want to spend time with them, so often you are getting up for those midnight feedings, only to arise at five the next morning to go to work. Interrupted sleep and minimal sleep were the norm for me. And when I was breastfeeding, there was the ever-present concern that the frozen milk supply would run low. I was constantly trying to navigate work and steal moments away between cases to pump. It was a daily battle. In anesthesia, often I covered three very busy, high-turnover operating rooms—seeing and evaluating patients preoperatively and readying them for the operating room. I had cases currently underway with intraoperative needs to manage and patients whose surgeries were complete but who were in the recovery phase. I also had teaching responsibilities if I was covering residents. In any free time, I was expected to be in the operating room going over anesthesia concepts or equations to calculate oxygen consumption. Finding time to pee, eat, and pump was not easy—and, some days, impossible.

Back in the fall of 2005, I'd had my third child in June and had just recently returned to clinical duties after my maternity leave. Every month there was a nighttime mandatory meeting for the business side of our practice unless you were on call.

It had been a long day. I had been running around the operating room nonstop, evaluating people preoperatively, alleviating anxiety, inducing anesthesia, caring for patients, waking patients up, and tucking patients into the recovery room, only to move on to the next patient. It was like a treadmill. No time for breaks, lunch, or peeing, and definitely no time for pumping. My breasts hurt. They were engorged. But I was running late. We were voting on a pretty important topic, and I wanted to get there. So off I ran. I was always trying to fulfill all obligations, despite my physical needs. My needs were last. (Every mom can relate to this!)

Midway through the meeting, across the table from me, a senior partner, number five in seniority, a man, whispered something to another male partner, also more senior than I. Both looked at me and chuckled. I was embarrassed and wondered what they could have said. Later, a female colleague who was in earshot of their inside joke told me what was muttered: "She could feed a small African nation with those bombs!"

I was mortified.

I was objectified.

I was sexualized.

And I was silent.

Afraid to say anything, afraid to call out this clear sexual harassment. I, a new partner, very junior in rank, just ignored them.

Later, I realized that these "comments" or "jokes," perhaps meant to be funny, were powerful. Words matter. They set a tone and influence culture, and thus what is deemed acceptable. An organization's culture consists of shared beliefs and values established by leaders and then communicated through various means and reinforced by acceptance from the masses. I was complicit in allowing this misogynistic culture to continue.

Culture at a workplace is a sensitive thing. It often takes on the feel from the predominant, most vocal group of individuals. In medicine, the hospital leaders and departmental chairs are responsible for setting the tone of the culture.

The boys club aspect of male culture can be communicated

literally in the words used throughout the organization, memos, and interdepartmental mail, as well as the behaviors permitted to exist. Take for instance the colloquial use of the terms "men" and "guys." "We'll need ten men to staff next weekend." "We need you guys to listen up." Or committee names like "manpower," which is in charge of overall staffing of the male, female, and nonbinary staff. Masculine language can make women and nonbinary individuals feel not excluded or shunned. It negates at least half of humanity. (Please allow a pause to let that sink in. Masculine language excludes over half of humanity!)

As groups grow larger and larger, direct personal communication is often infeasible. Therefore, departmental email very well may be the cornerstone of how important news is disseminated: new protocols for renal transplant care, alerts regarding drug shortages, announcements of when JCAHO (Joint Commission on Accreditation of Healthcare Organizations) is in-house. All very important matters are communicated through departmental email.

So a departmental email from our chair with important news and then a cartoon drawing of an upside-down snowman with remarks on what should be his eyes and nose yet looks like male genitalia was striking. Later, another offensive email showing an older female nurse injecting a needle into a buxom woman's boobs with the caption, "Sometimes you need to know when it's time to retire" also was sent throughout our entire department, to hundreds of people. The locker room, fraternity atmosphere was more and more entrenched than ever.

At least there was one thing our chair did equally: He was an equal opportunist in using both male and female sexual reproductive organs for entertainment purposes. Uncomfortable, right? And unprofessional.

These demeaning, sexist jokes and comments, humiliating

cartoons, and use of the default male in language all work to reinforce the boys club culture and the expectation that women will just acquiesce to it.

WALKING THE FLOOR AS A WOMAN

The operating room is high intensity. Some days, in some cases, the margins of life and death are not very far apart. The roles are defined. Often likened to a ship, the surgeon is known as the captain. They set the tempo, the pace, meticulously calling out the start with "incision" and dictating the end, when they see fit to start the closing sequences. The operating room is also where the hospital ideally wants maximum efficiency because it is here where the money is made.

Surgeons are paid salaries but often may also have incentives or higher bonuses if they "produce" more, or generate more RVUs (relative value units). (Yes, unfortunately, medicine is a business, now more than ever.) So completing surgeries quickly and efficiently, having turnover times low or staggering, and moving the following case into another open operating room are ideal for revenue generation, as well as getting cases done.

Classically, surgeons were male, as were most doctors. Some fields still are overwhelmingly male: orthopedics, neurosurgery, urology. Women surgeons have to exert authority to assume that captain role yet need to maintain their approachability or risk being seen as a b*tch.

There is a captain outside the OR as well. Someone who is overseeing the flow of cases, allocating personnel between rooms, and ensuring, as best as possible, the flow is seamless. This position is often an anesthesiologist, and I often had the opportunity to perform, or be tortured by, this task. We were called "floorwalkers."

For a floorwalker, there are multiple nonaligned goals to achieve at any one time. Above all, they keep things moving forward, but they also give breaks, assign staff to the next day's operations, assist any colleagues who need any help, and function as the liaison between surgeons and OR staff, among other tasks. At our Level 1 trauma center, emergencies arrived at our doorstep every day. These "add-on" cases needed immediate attention and thus "bumped" cases that were scheduled. The floorwalker did that as well. Those patients who had their cases "bumped" were often grumpy (and starving) and their surgeons even more displeased. The task of mediating these tensions and keeping the peace was a continual challenge.

Being impartial and fair to all was the goal. Yet we are all human and errors occur.

Just as a parent, a coach, or anyone who manages multiple people knows, it's hard not to show favorites and to maintain impartiality at all times. Some surgeons routinely approached the OR desk and the floorwalker and asked for a second room, again to stagger and maximize their efficiency. Their ability to stagger typically meant another surgeon could not access that room and thus was delayed. What became noticeable to many was that certain surgeons were shown favoritism and often got an extra room. Others not so much.

One day I was the floorwalker, and a certain female surgeon approached the desk and asked if she could have an open room, as her case had been bumped for an emergency.

The desk responded with a curt, "Why? Do you have to get home to your kids?"

I never heard that said to a male surgeon when he asked to get an extra room. Also, so what if it was because they wanted to get home, and so what if they wanted to see their kids? Why is that a bad thing? Everyone has a personal life.

This is an example of when a woman's commitment to her job is questioned because she has a family. This is a form of bias that persists in the workplace, subtly undermining women's authority and contributions. The expectation for women to balance the demands of their professional roles with their responsibilities at home creates a double bind that often leads to unjust scrutiny and evaluation of their commitment. This bias can manifest in various ways, from overt comments about personal lives to the insidious undercurrents of favoritism that benefit male counterparts.

This scenario reflects a larger societal issue where women are often perceived through a lens of traditional roles, leading to assumptions that their professional ambitions are secondary to their family obligations. Such attitudes not only perpetuate inequality but also contribute to a hostile environment in which women must constantly navigate their careers while proving their worth in a male-dominated field.

DAD'S VERSUS MOM'S RESPONSIBILITIES

Do working dads face the same level of criticism for balancing a career and family life? It's unlikely. Rarely are fathers accused of "prioritizing family over work" or pressured to cook dinner after a long day. Instead, dads often receive praise for actions that are considered baseline expectations for moms. For example, when a father drives his kids to school once a week, he's seen as a devoted parent. Meanwhile, when a mother does the school run the other four days, it's seen as just part of her role. Similarly, when a dad volunteers for a field trip, he's applauded, but when a mom does the same, it's merely assumed she's fulfilling her duties.

This disparity reflects a broader cultural bias that disproportionately credits fathers for meeting minimal parenting standards while holding mothers to impossibly high expectations. A father who brings a takeout dinner home after a long workday is labeled "fun," whereas a mother who does the same may be criticized for shirking her cooking responsibilities. Fathers who work eighty hours a week are seen as providing for their families, but when mothers do the same, they are often accused of neglecting their children.

Please, people. We do not live in the nineteenth century. Women can be the breadwinners, and dads can be expected to do more than just write checks (or fill in autopay) for groceries and the mortgage.

The reality is that gender roles in parenting remain deeply entrenched, even though society has progressed in many ways. A 2023 Pew Research Center report highlights significant disparities in how mothers and fathers perceive and share parenting responsibilities.[67] In opposite-sex relationships, 78 percent of mothers report doing more than their partners to manage their children's schedules, compared to just 54 percent of fathers. Similar gaps exist in helping with homework (65 percent versus 38 percent) and providing emotional support (58 percent versus 33 percent). Yet fathers are more likely to view these tasks as being shared equally, which suggests a disconnect between perception and reality.

Notably, mothers who take on a disproportionate share of childcare are more likely to say parenting is harder than they expected. Two-thirds of mothers (66 percent) report that parenting is harder than they expected, with 30 percent stating it is "a lot harder"—10 percentage points higher than fathers. Mothers, compared with fathers, are also more likely to describe parenting as tiring (47 percent versus 34 percent) and stressful (33 percent versus 24 percent) most of the time.

These challenges are compounded by societal judgment. Mothers are significantly more likely than fathers to feel judged for their parenting decisions by a variety of sources, including their own parents (47 percent versus 38 percent), in-laws (45 percent versus 37 percent), friends (34 percent versus 22 percent), and even online communities (31 percent versus 16 percent).[68] Such scrutiny not only adds emotional strain but also reinforces the pervasive expectation that mothers meet impossibly high standards in both their personal and professional lives.

The conclusion of this study is that women have more household responsibilities, and men think that the division of labor is equal when it isn't. Further, moms are more stressed, tired, judged, and anxious than their male partners. These pressures amplify the mental and emotional strain on women, which also affects their physical health over time.

Like I said earlier in the chapter, everyone has a personal life. So why do women have so many more responsibilities, stressors, and judgment associated with theirs?

For me, all the misogynistic comments and assumptions that came from being a woman in a male-dominated workplace were exacerbated by motherhood. The physical changes my body underwent, the shifting expectations regarding my schedule, and the redistribution of responsibilities all became fodder for scrutiny and judgment. Colleagues commented on my appearance, speculated about my commitment based on my parenting choices, and made light of the emotional toll that motherhood exacted. The tension between my professional obligations and the pull of having a newborn at home fueled a pervasive guilt that felt insurmountable. A working mother's guilt is profound. The feeling that no matter where you are or what you are doing, you are not in the right spot. If at work, you feel you should be home, and if at home, you feel like you are abandoning work. Physically you cannot be in two places at once, yet you're constantly wondering if you are in the right place. The guilt of missing events, not being the one to get the kids up in the morning or make them breakfast, and not making the mommy-and-me tea party compounds the feeling that you are doing motherhood wrong. It certainly doesn't help if you are made to feel equally flawed with your work choices. This environment was not only unsupportive, but it seemed to reinforce the idea that motherhood was a liability rather than a valued experience.

Ultimately, these judgments were not merely about my individual choices but rather a manifestation of a deeper, systemic misogyny that continues to permeate the culture of medicine. Motherhood was wielded as a weapon to penalize women, casting them as less dedicated or capable simply because they dared to embrace the dual roles of mother and professional. In a world that often refuses to acknowledge the complexities of women's lives, it became painfully clear that the challenges of motherhood were just another flavor of misogyny—a reminder that despite our best efforts, the workplace culture often remains rigidly entrenched in outdated norms that do little to support or uplift those who are balancing the demands of both work and family—both moms and dads alike.

TAKEAWAYS

1. **Motherhood changes the flavors of misogyny that women already face:** Before motherhood, I was seen as the "young, naive Blondilocks." After I became a mother, the stereotypes shifted: By some I was seen as a "lactating free rider" with big boobs who supposedly used her babies as excuses to shirk work responsibilities. These harmful narratives highlight how misogyny evolves and adapts to target women at different stages of life.
2. **You cannot control how others respond to your pregnancy and child-rearing decisions:** People will have opinions—often unsolicited—about your choices as a parent, from how you handle pregnancy to your methods of raising children. Recognize that their reactions reflect their biases, not your worth or decisions. Focus on making choices that align with your values and circumstances.
3. **Working mothers face guilt (internalized and external):** This guilt stems from the impossible double bind of feeling like you're failing both as a professional and as a parent. Society often reinforces this by holding working mothers to unrealistic standards in both domains. Combat this by giving yourself grace: You are doing the best you can. Avoid comparing your parenting choices to others', as every family's situation is different. Likewise, resist judging other mothers' decisions—everyone is navigating their unique challenges.

CHALLENGES TO YOU

1. **Understand your legal rights as a mother:** Research your workplace's obligations and policies related to motherhood. For example, is your company required to provide lactation spaces and breaks? Know your health benefits, including the details of your maternity or paternity leave. If you're a medical resident, investigate whether your specialty allows parental leave without extending your training period, as this varies. Being informed empowers you to advocate for yourself effectively.
2. **Sit down with your partner to evaluate responsibilities:** Have an open conversation—or even create a written plan—with your partner about how you divide responsibilities. This includes household management, childcare, and other shared tasks. Does the division feel equitable? It's OK if it's not a perfect 50/50 split, as different life circumstances (e.g., job demands) can influence the balance. However, an unequal distribution should never be assumed. Advocate for fairness, and don't hesitate to ask your partner for support when you need it.

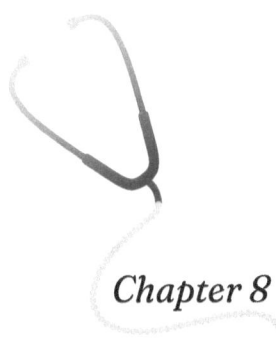

Chapter 8

DEMOTION AS NEUTRALIZATION

"I can be changed by what happens to me. But I refuse to be reduced by it."

—MAYA ANGELOU[69]

Throughout my career I continuously put myself out there, realizing that positions or advancements were not just going to be given to me. I nominated myself for positions on our governing body as well as committees and was "popular" enough to get elected. Because let's be real: These elections were not based on abilities but almost always on likability. Luckily, I was "liked" by my partners, probably because I never batted an eye or made a fuss about the "good old boys" vernacular, and as such, I managed to work my way or elect my way into some positions of relative power.

But in an academic institution, the ultimate power was in the chair's hands. He (and I choose that pronoun specifically because as I stated, I have only ever had male chairs) had the ability to form new committees or positions, reconstitute old committees, promote or demote people, dole out coveted non-clinical time, advance names for professorship titles, and even determine who was scheduled at the hospital he was the chair at. He also was in the rooms with the hospital C-suite executives and could speak highly of you or not. It was good to have him on your side. But after the "perky" meeting, I found myself not in his good graces.

I was methodically taken out of all my leadership positions. I was stripped of my chair position of committees, like the Critical Incident Committee, which I had chaired for over fifteen years. This committee oversees cases that have had an event happen that triggers an automatic review. I helped develop a reporting process and honed a great group of individuals who took pride in this work, as it led to system improvements for overall patient care. The hospital risk and quality improvement vice president often asked me or the committee to look at specific cases and depended on our committee to alert them of issues within the operating room arena. We had gained respect and admiration throughout the hospital for a superb quality review process. When my chair decided to "fire" me as chair of this committee, he stated that the committee was not performing and generating enough grand rounds for educational purposes, so it needed new leadership. It didn't matter that the computer system was being upgraded so cases were not being reported to the committee in a timely fashion. It was an excuse to rid me of my lead title and chair of the committee position. Suffice it to say, the next two chairs, who lasted less than a few years each, produced even fewer grand rounds lectures than when I led the team but were never fired for underperformance.

My mental health was suffering. I was crying almost nightly. I was walking on eggshells, feeling like any misstep was going to lead to another summons to the chair's office. I was not only not being promoted, but I was being actively demoted.

Another role that I had gained and loved was being a floorwalker. I discussed the importance of this role in the last chapter. The hospital operating room is a hectic place. There are scheduled cases, and then there are emergencies of all different acuities which need triaging. Some need immediate access to an operating arena; others can wait. Every surgeon thinks their case is the most pressing. Juggling cases is a full-time job, done by the floorwalker. It can be overwhelming, but as a mom of four, multitasking is a superpower I had.

I loved floorwalking, and I was good at it. I was repeatedly ranked as the best or one of the best. Many of the operating room nursing leaders and surgeons requested me to do more of it because of my skill.

My chair, claiming that I "did not support leadership" and therefore couldn't be seen as a leader, removed me from this role as well. By this point, I had been stripped of all my committee positions, my committee chair roles, and my position as a floorwalker. I also was routinely scheduled off-site, out of the primary hospital—ostracized to outpatient realms, where my ICU expertise certainly was not being utilized.

I finally had it.

I was removed from the resident interviewing committee, and another "token" female replaced me. I was removed from my floorwalker position and soon found myself scheduled more and more out of the major hospital I had practiced predominantly at for two decades. Instead of being at the trauma hospital, where my expertise in critical care medicine would be utilized, I was often scheduled at ambulatory surgical settings. Don't get me wrong; I enjoyed those hospitals, surgeons, and colleagues, and those days were a nice respite from the hectic, often pedal-to-the-metal days at the trauma center. But it also was a means to marginalize me. I was specifically put at the "outside" facilities so as to be "neutralized." I had very limited contact with my partners, as I worked solo. I had limited visibility in the group and limited interactions with the powerful executives at the larger academic hospital. I was ostracized.

Suddenly, new positions were created: vice chair of academics, floorwalker lead, OR director for anesthesia. Most of these positions were not posted as potential job openings. There was no stated selection process. No transparency. Out-of-the-blue announcements were made as to who would be given these new titles, accompanied with nonclinical time and power over others. It came as no surprise that these positions were all filled by white men.

OK, so let's break down this story. There are two phenomena going on here at the same time. The first is the demotion of me, an outspoken woman who challenged the way my boss ran things. And the second is the promotion of white men in leadership roles that I formerly occupied or that popped out of thin air.

Let's start with the first.

THE DEMOTION OF THE SQUEAKY WHEEL

Most industries, corporations, and workplaces function in a hierarchical manner. There is a leader or boss and those who answer to them or who are under them. A leader exists to maintain order and obedience, organizing multiple people to work toward a common goal in the most efficient manner possible. I don't need to tell you this; you probably live it, or at least have lived it in some part of your life.

But where things get interesting is what happens when that authority figure is challenged. Perhaps they don't delegate fairly. Perhaps they aren't doing things in the most efficient manner. Perhaps they are disliked. Perhaps they say something misogynistic. A worker beneath them respectfully says something. A "good" boss will take this feedback or helpful suggestion under consideration, as they know the comment was made to improve the group and they value the input of their coworkers. However, a "bad" boss might think the worker is not respecting their authority. In this situation, the bad boss needs to regain control and remind everyone of the hierarchy. The bad boss can use their power from their position of authority to suppress a dissenting voice. This boss can make an example of the worker, stripping them of their titles, responsibility, and visibility within the workplace. These actions are known as "symbolic power" or "symbolic domination." This tactic reinforces a hierarchy by making it clear who has the power to influence the work environment.

This is exactly what happened to me in my workplace. My chair didn't like that I made suggestions to his leadership plan. He didn't like that not only did I not laugh at his misogynistic emails, but I told others how inappropriate they were. He didn't like that I "talked back" to him during our "perky" conversation. In his mind, I needed to be reminded that he still pulled the strings. So he demoted me to show me who was boss, literally.

Putting gender back into the conversation, this reaction is an example of gendered organizational behavior. Studies suggest that women are often penalized more than men for challenging authority in male-dominated fields, as they're seen as "disrupting" the traditional power dynamic.[70] My chair's behavior perhaps stemmed from a discomfort with a female subordinate who was perceived as questioning his authority, prompting him to retaliate in ways intended to reinforce traditional gender roles. He could do this one of two ways: benevolent sexism (which may seem positive or protective but actually reinforces gender stereotypes and inequality) or hostile sexism (overtly negative and aggressive, often with the intent to dominate, belittle, or directly undermine). It's pretty clear that he demonstrated hostile sexism in my case.

TYPES OF SEXISM IN THE WORKPLACE

Benevolent Sexism

Benevolent sexism involves attitudes or behaviors that seem positive or protective but actually reinforce gender stereotypes and inequality.

"Protective" Measures:
A male boss might assume that certain projects are too challenging or high-stakes for female employees and assign them to male colleagues instead, thinking he's "protecting" them from stress or failure.

Exclusion from Certain Activities:
Inviting only men to certain social or networking events, such as after-work drinks or golf outings, under the guise that women wouldn't be interested or would feel uncomfortable, limits women's access to career-building opportunities.

Overly Complimentary Remarks:
Comments on a woman's appearance in a way that seems positive but distracts from her skills and professionalism. For example, a manager might frequently compliment female employees on their outfits or say they "brighten up the office," suggesting their primary value is aesthetic.

Hostile Sexism

Hostile sexism is overtly negative and aggressive, often with the intent to dominate, belittle, or directly undermine.

Direct Demotion or Retaliation:
A male boss demoting a female who questioned him is a clear example of hostile sexism, as it reflects a power move designed to silence and diminish a woman's influence and authority.

Inappropriate Comments and Sexual Objectification:
Allowing or making comments about a woman's body, like how colleagues remarked on my breasts, falls under hostile sexism. It objectifies and sexualizes women in the workplace, undermining their professionalism and making the environment uncomfortable or intimidating.

Inappropriate or Suggestive Emails:
Sending unprofessional, misogynistic emails or jokes contributes to a hostile work culture where women are not respected as equal colleagues.

Isolation or Sabotage:
Excluding women from important meetings or projects as a way to marginalize their influence or outright sabotage their work reflects hostile sexism aimed at undermining their professional success.

So why would he do this? Well, we can look at a psychological framework for that. He could perhaps have a narcissistic leadership style, which gives him an inflated sense of worth. Leaders with narcissistic traits can be hypersensitive to perceived challenges to their authority, often taking extreme measures to "punish" those who question them. This type of leadership can lead to punitive behavior toward subordinates as a way for the leader to restore their self-image and reestablish control. He could also operate with a fear-based leadership style. This style, characterized by retaliating against anyone perceived as a threat to the leader's control or reputation, can stem from an insecure attachment to power. This perspective sees the need to put others "in their place" as a way to manage internal fears of being seen as weak.

We could also look at it from a sociological perspective. Sociologically, demotion and isolation are classic methods of silencing individuals who question authority. This approach serves to isolate both physically and socially, reducing the perpetrator's influence within the workplace. This tactic also often involves gaslighting, where the person in power not only demotes the individual but may imply or state that they're doing it for the subordinate's own good or that the subordinate "doesn't understand" the broader needs of the organization, creating self-doubt and further silencing dissent. These steps become necessary for the leader to maintain control and discourage others from following suit in voicing dissent. By demoting me, my boss probably intended to set an example, showing others the cost of stepping out of line.

Ultimately, there's no way to know why he acted the way he did, nor does it really matter. But I think understanding these types of things helped me rationalize what happened to me. Understanding that his actions were rooted in systemic, often (although certainly not always) gendered, biases—not personal failings—allowed me to view this experience as part of a larger issue that can affect anyone who challenges established hierarchies.

THE PROMOTION OF...MORE WHITE MEN?

This second facet, the quiet promotion of friends and male peers, reveals a common yet often overlooked issue in hiring and promotions: affinity bias, or the similar-to-me effect. In my workplace, this took the form of new, unseen managerial positions that went to a select group of individuals—white men who happened to be personal friends or at least allies of my chair. There were no open application processes, no job postings, and certainly no transparent qualifications for these roles.

Affinity bias is a cognitive shortcut that often compels us to gravitate toward people who remind us of ourselves in some way.[71] While this can seem innocuous or even positive in everyday social settings, it has significant implications when applied to professional environments, especially where people in power hold sway over others' positions, opportunities, and livelihoods.

Here's a non-workplace example of affinity bias that I've noticed in my own life. In my family, we have two standard poodles who we love dearly for their fluffy coats, (supposedly) easy trainability, and snuggly, affectionate nature. I didn't grow up with poodles, but my husband did, so my love for the breed is newer, from my adult life. Now, whenever we walk in the park and see another poodle, we get super excited. We walk up to them, pet their curly hair, strike up a conversation with the family, and chat excitedly. I don't have the same excitement when we come across golden retrievers or Great Danes. This is a more benign example of affinity bias that makes me more apt to engage with fellow poodle families because they are more likely to remind me of my own family and dogs. We all have our own version of this type of bias; we can't help it!

Affinity bias becomes a problem when it enters the workplace and affects the opportunities of others. In hiring or promoting, affinity bias encourages leaders to favor those who share their characteristics, backgrounds, or ways of thinking. For example, a leader might consciously or unconsciously select candidates who mirror their own demographics, such as race, gender, or age, assuming that these individuals will "fit in" better or bring "trusted" qualities to the role. Men are more likely to hire men. White people are more likely to hire white people. People from Georgia are more likely to hire people from Georgia. It's comforting to hire someone who reminds you of a younger version of you.

And so the demographics of people who are leaders remain relatively the same. Historically, this tendency has reinforced exclusionary practices. When unchecked, affinity bias stifles diversity, reinforces homogeneity, and limits the workplace's potential for growth and innovation.[72]

BIASES & EFFECTS THAT HELP EXPLAIN WHY LEADERSHIP (& INDUSTRIES) ARE HOMOGENOUS

Affinity Bias

Affinity bias draws us toward people who reflect our own characteristics, views, or values. It gives you the feeling of "helping someone who you see yourself in" or a "younger version of you." This can also manifest as helping people who we see are a part of our "in-group." For instance, favoring someone who grew up in your hometown or who graduated from your alma mater; you already see them as someone in your community, so you favor them for hire or promotion, or even just as a conversationalist. This is why we have friends who are similar to us in terms of backgrounds, interests, values, education, appearance, and more.

Status Quo Bias

This is the tendency to prefer things to stay the same, especially in established systems or power structures. People often unconsciously resist change or overlook diverse candidates because they feel safer maintaining a familiar or "tried and true" structure.

Confirmation Bias

Confirmation bias further compounds the issue by causing individuals to seek information that reinforces their existing beliefs or stereotypes. If my chair believed that his male friends were natural leaders or fit his image of "ideal" team members, he might unconsciously ignore evidence to the contrary. When people only notice information that confirms their beliefs, they create an echo chamber that makes it difficult to consider differing perspectives or talents.

The Halo Effect (includes pretty privilege)

The halo effect leads us to generalize a single positive quality about someone—such as attractiveness—across their entire character or abilities. In hiring, this can mean that someone perceived as physically appealing is also assumed to be intelligent, hardworking, friendly, and a strong candidate overall. Conversely, those who don't fit conventional standards of attractiveness may be seen as less capable or likable. This bias, which is influenced by factors such as appearance, age, body type, and race, tends to disproportionately impact women.

In reflecting on my own experience, it's clear that many of the "hidden" promotions I observed weren't just instances of nepotism; they were also examples of affinity bias at work. As long as unchecked biases shape our workplaces, those in power will continue to reinforce traditional dynamics—often at the expense of fair opportunity.

THE IMPORTANCE OF DIVERSE VOICES AND PERSPECTIVES

Diverse voices and perspectives are essential in creating a fuller, more nuanced understanding of the challenges and needs we face, both in professional settings and in society at large. When we engage with individuals from different backgrounds, identities, and experiences, we gain insight into issues that we may otherwise overlook, as each person's point of view adds richness and depth to the conversation. This diversity of thought helps us approach problems from multiple angles, uncovering blind spots that may exist in more homogeneous groups.

In fields like medicine, where decisions can directly impact people's lives, the importance of diverse perspectives becomes even more pronounced. When the voices of patients with diverse identities—whether based on gender, race, ethnicity, socioeconomic status, or other factors—are not fully represented in the healthcare workforce, there is a risk of overlooking their unique needs and concerns. Medical professionals who all share similar backgrounds may unintentionally miss the specific cultural, social, or health-related factors that affect patients from different communities. This lack of understanding can result in a narrower approach to patient care that does not address the complexities of their experiences.

My daughter experienced this firsthand during a Wilderness Advanced First Aid course, where she was by far the youngest participant at just eighteen years old and one of the only women in the class. She needed the certification for her summer job leading canoeing and hiking trips for teenage girls. Meanwhile, many of her classmates were burly middle-aged men who required the certification to work on electrical lines in remote areas.

During one exercise, the instructor divided the class into two groups: one group acted as patients, each given a set of symptoms to act out, while the other group played the role of first aid responders, tasked with diagnosing and treating the "patients." As a first aid responder, my daughter came across one of the few other women in the class, who was describing severe abdominal pain. After asking just two preliminary questions, my daughter quickly inquired about her patient's menstrual cycle and was able to diagnose the issue as severe menstrual cramps.

Later, during the debrief, the class learned that every female first responder and only one male first responder had correctly diagnosed the patient. Many of the male responders hadn't even considered asking about her period, and one admitted that although he had thought about it, he'd felt too shy to bring it up, fearing it would make the patient uncomfortable.

This exercise was a valuable learning moment for the men in the class, and it highlights an important lesson about representation in medicine. Male providers undergo years of training to ensure they ask the right questions and provide thorough care to all patients, and many deliver excellent medical care to women. The lesson here is not that male doctors cannot treat female patients—history has shown that they can and do.

The real takeaway is that lived experience can shape medical intuition. My daughter, as a woman who had personally experienced period pain, was able to quickly recognize the symptoms and ask the right questions. Her shared identity with the patient provided her with an instinctive understanding that many of her male classmates lacked.

This is why we need diverse doctors—not just in gender but across race, ethnicity, socioeconomic background, disability, and sexual orientation. A more diverse medical workforce means a broader range of perspectives, experiences, and insights, which leads to more informed questioning, better diagnoses, and improved patient care. Doctors from underrepresented backgrounds may recognize health disparities sooner, understand cultural concerns more deeply, and be better equipped to build trust with patients who share their experiences.

Promoting diverse doctors and leaders isn't about enacting DEI practices for the sake of seeming progressive or woke. It's about ensuring that every patient has a doctor who understands them—not just through textbooks but through shared life experience. Diverse doctors are more likely to be attuned to subtle but critical symptoms of diverse patients, leading to faster, more accurate diagnoses.

This gap in understanding isn't just theoretical; it has real, life-or-death consequences.

Take heart attacks in women, for example. Heart disease is the number one killer of women, yet many healthcare providers default to the "classic" male symptom: chest pain radiating to the jaw and arm. In reality, women's heart attack symptoms often present differently, with nausea, shortness of breath, or fatigue. Because these symptoms don't fit the standard (i.e., male) symptoms, women are more likely to have their heart attacks misdiagnosed or dismissed.

The issue extends far beyond gender. A 2023 *JAMA* article estimated that 795,000 patients in hospitals die or are permanently disabled each year due to medical errors or misdiagnoses.[73] Moreover, patients from racial and ethnic minorities are 20–30 percent more likely to be misdiagnosed than white patients. One significant factor is the lack of racial diversity among physicians. Doctors from underrepresented backgrounds bring lived experience that can help them recognize symptoms in ways that others might overlook. A physician who has personally seen how conditions present on darker skin is more likely to diagnose certain illnesses correctly. While I can't speak from this perspective as a white doctor, I can recognize its necessity in improving healthcare equity.

Equally important is the diversity of medical education and training materials. The resources used to teach future doctors often fail to represent the full spectrum of patients doctors will treat. Medical textbooks and training materials often depict diseases and medical conditions through the lens of the "seventy-kilo white male" patient, failing to reflect the diverse ways conditions may manifest in different populations. From a study done in 2018, only 4–5 percent of medical images in the top four anatomy textbooks taught in medical school depict dark skin, and even among those, 75 percent are on the lighter end of the spectrum.[74] This underrepresentation can lead to misdiagnosis and delayed treatment, particularly in dermatology, infectious diseases, and emergency medicine.

For example, many skin conditions, such as Lyme disease, eczema, and skin cancer, present differently on darker skin. A bull's-eye rash, commonly associated with Lyme disease, may be less visible or appear differently on melanated skin. Similarly, erythema (redness), a key sign of inflammation or infection, often looks deep purple or violet on melanated skin rather than the bright red doctors are taught to recognize on paler skin. Without proper exposure to images of these conditions on diverse skin tones, clinicians may fail to diagnose them accurately, leading to poorer patient outcomes.

Recognizing this gap, Chidiebere Ibe, a Nigerian medical illustrator, has been at the forefront of increasing representation in medical illustrations.[75] His viral image of a Black fetus in a medical diagram drew attention to the issue and sparked a much-needed conversation in the medical community. Ibe has worked with organizations such as Harvard Medical School's International Center for Genetic Diseases and Illustrate Change, a project aimed at incorporating more diverse illustrations into medical education.

Similarly, projects like WoundWatch (which specializes in wound care) and the Reframing Revolution (which specializes in women's and reproductive health) have been creating royalty-free, diverse medical image collections, showcasing conditions across a range of skin tones, body types, and gender identities.[76] These initiatives ensure that future doctors and medical students become accustomed to diagnosing conditions on all skin colors and body types.

Beyond diagnosis, representation in medical illustrations also impacts patient trust and engagement. Studies suggest that when patients see themselves represented in medical materials and their identities reflected in the people helping treat them, they feel more understood and are more likely to engage with their healthcare providers.[77] The historical lack of diversity in medical illustrations has contributed to mistrust of the healthcare system, particularly in Black and Indigenous communities, where medical racism has left lasting scars.

Diversity in medicine isn't just about who is practicing; it's also about the tools and resources they rely on. Without medical images that accurately depict conditions across different racial, ethnic, and gender backgrounds, even the most well-intentioned doctors may struggle to provide equitable care. Incorporating diverse illustrations in medical education is just as essential as increasing diversity within the medical workforce. When physicians are trained with inclusive diagnostic materials, they are better equipped to recognize symptoms across all patients, reducing misdiagnoses and improving outcomes. Diversity in medicine is not just a moral imperative; it's a practical necessity. It leads to more effective, compassionate, and equitable healthcare for everyone.

TAKEAWAYS

1. **Learn to recognize hierarchical behaviors and symbolic domination:** Gendered hierarchical behaviors, though often subtle, are powerful tools for maintaining control and neutralizing those who challenge authority. This chapter demonstrates how leaders—particularly in male-dominated industries—use tactics such as demotion, silencing, and stripping responsibilities to remind subordinates of their subordinate status. These actions, though they may seem minor or temporary, reinforce the power dynamics that diminish the voice and influence of individuals, especially women, who question the established order. Recognizing these behaviors is the first step in reclaiming one's position and protecting professional integrity within the organization.

2. **Affinity bias plays a role in workplace promotions:** Affinity bias—our subconscious tendency to favor individuals who resemble us in terms of background, gender, race, or other characteristics—plays a significant role in workplace promotions and decision-making processes. Such biases can result in the promotion of individuals based on personal connections rather than merit or qualifications. The perpetuation of homogeneity in

leadership roles not only stifles diversity but also reinforces exclusionary practices that prevent diverse voices from reaching decision-making positions. Awareness of this bias is crucial for fostering a fair and inclusive workplace where promotions are based on competency rather than personal likeness.

3. **Intersectionality is powerful in workplace dynamics:** Intersectionality helps us understand how multiple aspects of identity—gender, race, class, sexuality, religion, ability, etc.—interact to create unique experiences of inequality. This awareness can be a powerful tool in addressing systemic challenges in the workplace.

4. **Diverse identities and experiences enhance medical intuition and patient care:** Diverse perspectives in medicine are not just about fairness; they improve diagnostic accuracy, patient trust, and treatment outcomes. When healthcare providers share identities or experiences with their patients, they are more likely to ask the right questions and recognize symptoms that others might overlook. Without diversity in the medical workforce and in educational materials, critical health disparities persist, leading to preventable misdiagnoses and poorer outcomes for underrepresented communities.

CHALLENGES TO YOU

1. **Audit your own bias in mentorship and promotions:** Reflect on the types of people who have helped you and who you have helped after you in your professional journey. Do they look like you? It's natural to feel a connection with those like you, but it's essential to recognize that affinity bias can skew your decisions. To foster inclusivity, make a conscious effort to mentor individuals from diverse backgrounds and perspectives.

2. **Advocate for transparent and inclusive promotion practices:** Evaluate your workplace's promotion process. Are decisions based on merit, or do personal connections and shared characteristics influence who gets promoted? Advocate for more transparent promotion practices that value competence, diverse experiences, and unique perspectives. If you notice patterns of homogeneity, speak up and suggest improvements to ensure fair and inclusive promotion pathways for all employees.

3. **Identify and bridge your knowledge blind spots:** There is always more to learn, and we are all lifelong learners. We all have areas of limited knowledge—whether due to personal experience, education, or exposure. The key to growth is recognizing these gaps and actively seeking ways to close them. This could mean reading diverse perspectives, engaging in conversations outside your usual circles, or seeking mentorship from those with different backgrounds. By identifying what you don't know and making a conscious effort to learn, you become more informed, adaptable, and effective in both professional and personal settings.

Chapter 9

ECHOES OF DISCONTENT

"Never doubt that a small group of thoughtful, committed citizens can change the world; indeed, it's the only thing that ever has."
—WIDELY ATTRIBUTED TO MARGARET MEAD

Back in 2018, when my hospital "did not renew" the contract of a prominent female surgeon, tension began to brew within the operating room arena. Many women became concerned that another female surgeon was leaving. It seemed like a pattern, with many female surgeons lasting only a short time and then moving on. Two female thoracic surgeons left in a fairly short period. Notably, they left not to retire or have a family but to take full-time positions elsewhere. Subsequently, another female thoracic surgeon came and went as well. A female pediatric surgeon, three female trauma surgeons, a female bariatric surgeon, and a female colorectal surgeon who trained at the institution and was one of the most senior surgeons at the institution left. Each one could perhaps be explained. But all of them? Ten female surgeons in perhaps five years. The "optics" for female surgeons at this institution were not good. To the credit of the institution, the chief medical officer called for a meeting. At this meeting were members of the anesthesia department, surgeons, the operating room nursing staff, operating room directors, chairs of surgery and anesthesia, and a female psychiatrist who had an interest in behavioral dynamics and conflict management.

To hear directly from female physicians who worked in the operating room realm, the psychiatrist held a meeting for all female physicians, both faculty and trainees, to come chat about their experiences. The meeting was deemed confidential, and initially, the objective was stated as an opportunity for all the women to hear stories of what it was like being a woman in the operating room. It was one of the most cathartic experiences of my life.

There were approximately forty of us in a room. Our moderator asked us to reflect on our experiences as physicians and write down on a Post-it note anytime we felt harassed, either with comments or behaviors. We were then instructed to silently place the notes on the walls around us. Initially, there was a hushed silence as we all wondered. Our names were not attached to the comments, but we were still visibly placing them on the wall for all the world to see. Concern of whether this was a "safe place" faded as one by one we all walked around placing our private incidents on the wall. These microaggressions and macroaggressions, which we all had shoved so far down to hopefully never have to think of again, were now out there. Every single one of us had an experience when we were called "honey" or "babe." We all recalled a time when we had a physical characteristic commented on in an inappropriate fashion. Stories of having butts slapped, literal propositions made, belittling side comments. It was one of those moments when, although you felt horrible for what happened to the other women, you also felt less alone. I felt solidarity. It was not me; it was not "my fault." All the second-guessing of "Did that really happen?" or "He didn't mean anything by that," or maybe "I'm making too much of this" disappeared. This was not my fault. I (and the other women) did not ask for this. We do not deserve this. There was power in our shared experience.

But had any of us reported it? Not a single one.

I was surprised, but then again, I wasn't.

I wanted a #MeToo uprising in medicine. For women physicians to band together, share their stories more publicly, and hold those in power accountable for their actions and discrimination. A national movement has yet to really take shape in the world of medicine. But why?

WHY DON'T WOMEN REPORT GENDER HARASSMENT OR DISCRIMINATION?

1. **Uncertainty About What Constitutes Harassment:** Many women don't report gender discrimination or harassment because they aren't sure if what they've experienced qualifies. Is it a joke dismissed as "funny"? A side glance? Being called by your first name while men are addressed as "Dr. Last Name"? Or an inappropriate email that no one else comments on? When no one else speaks up, it's easy to question whether it's truly harassment.
2. **Lack of Clear Definitions and Training:** There's little training or consensus on what constitutes discrimination or harassment. Without clear definitions, it can be difficult to determine if you can even prove what happened. Did anyone else hear them call me "baby"?

3. **Unclear Reporting Channels:** How do you report harassment? Who do you go to, especially if the instigator is in a powerful position? If the person responsible controls your work opportunities, the stakes are even higher. Reporting can seem like a career risk. In my case, he was my chair and in charge of valuable nonclinical time with the power to demote me off committees and positions of power, like floorwalking.
4. **Distrust of HR and Reporting Systems:** HR (human resources) often prioritizes the institution over the individual. Frequently, individuals describe having limited confidence in HR and formal reporting systems based on actual experiences with reporting, experiences from other individuals who have reported, and general perceptions of the reporting systems. The biggest concern for most employees was that reporting would result in no "meaningful action" to address the situation and perpetrator despite the reporter dedicating a significant amount of time and emotional investment to go through the lengthy and arduous process.
5. **Fear of Minimization and Dismissal:** Women fear that their concerns will be minimized. I experienced this firsthand when I raised the issue of unequal compensation and was told, "You must have it wrong; he's such a good guy." These kinds of comments signal allegiance to the perpetrator and protect him while undermining the woman's experience, as discussed in a 2022 *Harvard Business Review* article titled "Stop Protecting 'Good Guys.'"[78]
6. **Fear of Retaliation:** The fear of retaliation is significant. Victims are often labeled as "squeaky wheels" or "not team players," making it harder to find jobs, get promotions, or avoid marginalization. Retaliation can range from career-

ending demotions to more subtle but equally harmful behaviors like cold shoulders and exclusion. It's a spectrum. In my case, there was a petition that didn't overtly name me, but everyone at that point knew it was me. The petition basically called me crazy, a liar, and an instigator of trouble. Someone who made things up for their own advantage and benefit. More on that later! And then the not-so-concrete but equally injurious, hushed conversations that quickly end when you walk in the room, the sideway glances, the walking right past you even though you've hung out together for over twenty years. The "you're not one of us anymore" actions that make you feel less than, or an outright outcast.

7. **Financial Barriers:** Hiring a lawyer is expensive. Institutions have in-house legal teams, while individuals must find and pay for employment law specialists. My lawyer's retainer was $10,000 just to start. Three years in, I shudder to think how much my lawyer's bill is up to at this point.

8. **Time and Stress:** The process of reporting is long and draining. Gathering evidence, reconstructing events, writing out what happened, finding emails and paper trails to corroborate your stories, and meeting with investigators takes months, even years. In my case, the hospital's investigation alone took nine months. During this time, the stress of acting normal at work while knowing my chair was under investigation was nearly unbearable. I had to maintain my "perkiness" and did not want to seem like I knew anything was happening since I filed my complaints confidentially.

9. **The Emotional Toll:** The emotional toll is immense. Reliving traumatic events during interviews and wondering where the investigation stands is exhausting. The stress seeps into personal life, affecting relationships and family time. More than three years of this has been emotionally and

physically draining, with ripple effects that have impacted my family in ways I can't undo. I did not want my children to worry about me, my job, or what financial repercussions might come. They didn't know what was happening, but they knew I was not fully present at times. There were summer vacation days when I'd leave our summer beach house, where extended family was all staying, to drive back to Portland and meet my lawyer. There were phone calls with my lawyer at night and on weekends and on days off meant to be family days and Zoom meetings while I was on vacation driving north but tuning in to hear the latest developments. There were countless moments that were spoiled secondary to the stress and drama. Time with my family and children I cannot get back.

Once you understand the numerous barriers to reporting, it becomes painfully clear why so many women, myself included, hesitate to come forward. The consequences of reporting can feel insurmountable, both personally and professionally. These obstacles create a system wherein women are left to endure mistreatment in silence, fearful of the consequences of speaking out.

This reluctance isn't a sign of weakness but a testament to the deeply flawed systems that prioritize protecting institutions over individuals. While there is immense strength in the solidarity women feel when sharing their stories, true change requires more than just speaking up—it requires dismantling the structures that make reporting feel like an impossible and costly battle. Institutional reform, transparent accountability processes, and a cultural shift that actively supports women must be at the forefront of this fight. We can't afford to continue losing talented women to a system that punishes those brave enough to stand up against it.

TAKEAWAYS

1. **Shared stories diminish isolation:** The power of shared experiences can't be overstated. When women came together to share their stories of harassment and discrimination, it was both cathartic and validating. This solidarity created a sense of community, reminding us that the problem was systemic—not personal.
2. **Reporting often feels impossible:** Women often don't report harassment due to unclear definitions, lack of trust in reporting systems, fear of retaliation, financial and emotional burdens, and the belief that no meaningful action will result. These barriers perpetuate a culture of silence and prevent accountability for harmful behavior.
3. **Institutions are prioritized over individuals:** Organizations often prioritize protecting their reputation over addressing discrimination, leaving victims unsupported. For real change, institutions must implement transparent accountability processes, prioritize victims' voices, and dismantle systems that discourage reporting.

CHALLENGES TO YOU

Take proactive steps to foster equity in your workplace or community. Reflect and act on the following exercises:

1. **Map your support system:** Identify allies or mentors you can trust and rely on when facing challenges. Building this network is key to navigating difficult situations.
2. **Define your boundaries:** Write down instances that made you uncomfortable or felt inappropriate, even if they seemed minor at the time. Understanding and defining harassment for yourself is the first step to recognizing patterns.
3. **Practice reporting scenarios:** Role-play reporting an issue with a trusted person to explore how you'd communicate your concerns. This will build confidence and clarify your thoughts.

Chapter 10

THE FINAL STRAW

"*I am no longer accepting the things I cannot change. I am changing the things I cannot accept.*"

—ANGELA DAVIS[79]

The intensive care unit is named so—intensive—for a reason. The sickest of the sick are there, and at the only Level 1 hospital in the state, our census is always large. The unfortunate who find themselves patients here are often involved in traumas or transferred from outside hospitals that no longer can meet their needs. They are often on ventilators or on multiple vasopressors and need recurrent surgeries to address their issues. They also need top-of-the-line nursing and subspecialty care. My weeks in the unit were long—typically eighty to ninety hours over the seven days.

We are caring for not only the patient but also their family, who so tirelessly comes to be by the bedside of their loved one, who participates in rounds with us, and who in their own way needs help and attention. We are lucky to have residents: surgical, anesthesia, and emergency physicians. Medical students from two well-respected institutions, along with physician assistants, nurse practitioners, pharmacists, pharmacy residents, occupational therapists, physical therapists, and nutritionists, are engaged in their respective programs. These future physicians and care team members are preparing to become the next generation of professionals we will someday entrust with our own care.

My weeks in the ICU were so incredibly rewarding. I *loved* it. I came alive, knowing that this was where I was meant to be. This was what all my training was for, to help these patients and to nurture these young learners. But at the end of each week, I was tired.

Like anywhere, there are politics involved in hospitals, and the ICUs are no different. Who "controls" the units? Is it an anesthesia-run unit, a surgical-run unit, or a pulmonary unit?

My training being in postsurgical and trauma units, I gravitated to a similar unit. In the hospital when I arrived, a colleague, also an anesthesia and intensive care–trained female physician, practiced in the surgical/trauma unit. I followed suit. For over a decade, she and I were the only two anesthesia-based ICU doctors in the hospital and in our practice. We single-handedly fostered the anesthesia residency-required ICU rotations and met all the ACGME-mandated requirements to continue to have an anesthesia residency program.

About ten years ago, our department and group decided to venture into cardiac ICUs, an arena that did not particularly interest me or my colleague; nor was I sufficiently trained in the particulars of the management of cardiac intensive care patients, who may require cardiac assist devices, ECMO, etc. My group, therefore, needed more personnel and hired physicians trained in that arena as well as in anesthesia. These soon-to-be partners happened to be all male. They also were at least fifteen years junior to my colleague and me. They began like we all did, working in the operating rooms as anesthesiologists and then eventually attending in the cardiac intensive care units. They, too, had long weeks. They logged similar hours and had a census typically half our size, so fewer patients, fewer families, and no learners. They had physician assistants who had worked in the units for many years. No teaching responsibilities, except perhaps a medical student who might elect to be on their service for observation and learning.

Because of the long hours, they petitioned our group for days off after their weeks in the ICU. Without boring you too much about the details, suffice it to say they got what they asked for. Two days off, every Monday and Tuesday, following their seven-day ICU week. As one senior male partner always said at practice meetings, "We have to keep the young bucks happy." Well, what about the two old does who had been performing those duties, and more, for over fifteen years? We approached leadership and inquired if we, too, would receive two days off after each of our weeks in the ICU.

"Absolutely not!" we were told. "What they are doing is so much harder. You're comparing apples to oranges."

What was the difference? ICU patients are ICU patients. All are on vents and require making critical management decisions continuously, tweaking vasoactive meds, addressing new complications, and working on multidiscipled teams. We also had teaching duties and more patients and families, and we were the primary attending, whereas our "young buck" colleagues were only consulting, as the cardiac surgeon remained the attending of record.

Still, it was a hard no.

* * *

My female colleague, the other intensive care medicine doctor in the trauma units, and I went to the "manpower" committee members. How ironic, right? Expecting the "manpower" team to address gender inequities when the name itself is non-inclusive. But that was the appropriate committee, I thought.

The charter of the committee is to address and ensure workplace call equity and work equity across all the subdivisions within the department and between all the staff, partners and non-partners. They addressed call allotments, vacation selections, holiday assignments, and the like and were responsible for granting the cardiovascular critical care doctors with time off after working their seven days on their intensive care shifts. I assumed that it was an oversight. And although my colleague and I had waited it out for over a year, we decided to finally seek to be treated as our male colleagues.

Unfortunately, it became apparent after chatting with members of the committee that they had no understanding of what my colleague and I did in the ICU, nor were they interested. They felt that the men "deserved" time off because their hours during their ICU week were long. When we pointed out that we worked the same hours, had similarly complex patients, and had a census that was typically larger than theirs, and we also had teaching responsibilities for residents and med students, something our male colleagues typically did not have, they didn't seem to care.

We then went to our chair. He reiterated that it was just different. We were comparing apples and oranges.

We went to our divisional governing body and they, too, saw

no need to grant the women the same time off that the men received despite performing the same job, just in a different ICU.

Getting nowhere, feeling exhausted and betrayed by our colleagues, we then sought help from the chair of critical care, an independent person outside our private practice. He, too, felt like he could not overrule our group's decision and thought it was an internal issue for us to deal with.

Back to our group, to the beginning. Having looked for help from committees, asking both chair and governing divisional leadership and getting nowhere, we then turned toward our chief medical officer and human resources leader. After a lengthy meeting, outlining the disparity between how the only two female ICU physicians were not receiving the same days off after working in the ICUs, a form of compensation that the male critical care doctors were receiving, we again got nowhere.

We were exhausted, defeated, and marginalized.

Our value was not recognized. Our work was inferior in their eyes. And so for over four years, for eight or so weeks a year, our male colleagues received two days off every week they worked in the ICU while my female partner and I received an early release on the Monday after working our grueling seven ICU days, relieving us of maybe three hours instead of two days.

In our group, compensation comes in two forms. The good old-fashioned way is money, and the other way is time. Time is money, we often said.

Well, that's a lot of days off that we should have had. Or if required to work, we should have been paid extra. Our male colleagues sometimes offered to work on the Monday or Tuesday after their ICU weeks. They received extra compensation for working those days, money my female partner and I never received. We never received the time or the money when working those days.

We petitioned our chair, a white man from the South. We petitioned the chair of the intensive care units, another white man. We met with our chief medical officer, also a white man. We met with the "manpower" committee chair, yet another white man. All of them flatly refused.

Diminishing and devaluing our work told us in an overt way that we were not valued to the same extent as our "young buck" colleagues were. The organization placed higher importance on keeping the new male ICU-boarded physicians "happy" rather than treating my colleague and me fairly. They refused to acknowledge that we were functioning in the same way as our male colleagues and thus deserving of the same compensation.

In March of 2020, the whole world turned upside down. COVID-19 was hitting the United States, and New England was not immune. It took a little longer to arrive, and thankfully, we did not see the pandemic crisis to the same extent that New York and other larger cities were dealing with, but sure enough, COVID-19 cases eventually came pouring in.

Our hospital redeployed space earmarked for other units and outfitted new ICU beds. We obviously needed more ICU resources, and all those trained and credentialed in ICU medicine were expected to help with staffing needs. I had always been part of the trauma/postsurgical units, as mentioned before. This was under the auspices of the surgical department, and I had an ICU director who I reported to as well as a surgeon who oversaw the entire acute care surgical service line. Conversely, my male ICU colleagues, who functioned in the cardiac ICUs, did so under the anesthesia department umbrella. Two separate service lines. Two different leadership structures.

When COVID-19 hit, I was obviously going to be utilized as part of the trauma ICU group, as I had worked under them for over twenty years. My chair, however, assumed I would be utilized with the anesthesia subgroup of intensivists, even though I had never worked beside them in the ICU capacity. This created conflict, as both might assign me units to cover at the same time. Trying to minimize the confusion, I sent an email to all involved, both the trauma leaders as well as my anesthesia leaders. This prompted my anesthesia chair to summon me to his office. Upon arrival, I was met not only by my chair but also by my practice director, our chief medical officer, and one of the young bucks who worked in the cardiac ICUs. It was an ambush.

All four decided to lambast me and chastise me for sending my inquiring email. My chair said that it "embarrassed" my young male colleague and that I "broke the chain of command" by including "outsiders," i.e., the trauma surgeons, in the email. Despite my best efforts to explain that I included them to avoid confusion and ensure coordination so that each group wouldn't assign me to the COVID-19 units simultaneously, they still didn't care.

Gender inequality and discrimination is insidious.

Small things like being called pet names such as "Blondilocks" or being gifted the cow doll were playful gestures that deprofessionalized me. I was invited to committees as the "token" female, while departmental emails celebrated a "manly man" contest, complete with cartoons depicting male genitalia and older women portrayed as inept. The workplace was designed to keep the "young bucks" happy, with women relegated to chairing the social committee and planning parties for over twenty years. Meetings were often set up to ambush and intimidate me when I was seen as not following the chain of command. On top of that, the gender pay gap persisted, with women not receiving the same compensatory time off as their younger male colleagues after working weeklong intensive care shifts. It all adds up.

Luckily for me, I started to see the big picture.

I was a strong woman who challenged the patriarchy. My chair did not like that I just did not "fall in line" and await "marching orders" from him.

I was finally exhausted by trying to look the other way at all these gendered events. I was tired of making allowances for bad behavior or comments and letting all these microaggressions and macroaggressions slide. I also realized that if I did not say or do anything, things were never going to change. I was sad for all the women to come. That this was still the state of medicine. They, too, would have to walk the tightrope of being nice but authoritative, but not too authoritative. I wanted to help fix it.

I was always taught never to just sit around upon seeing an injustice. But to act on it. To bring it to light so it could be corrected.

So I did. Luckily, I have friends in faraway places who knew of my chair's prior behavior. Apparently, he was a good old boy from the South who was used to getting his way. He had been handed jobs from his male network of friends. Moving up the hospital ladder and eventually landing a chair position is definitely easier when the initial stepping stones are handed out by those who look like you and act like you. Unfortunately, he had made some enemies at his last job, where he was being investigated for sexual harassment. Apparently, he was chair of the department when a certified nurse anesthetist (CRNA) complained about one of the male anesthesia physicians who was hitting on her. Per the narrative shared with me, instead of investigating the situation or reprimanding the male doctor, he saw fit to just remove the CRNA from the operating room and ostracize her to the pre-op clinic. This move was not welcome by her and was seen as punitive for coming forward with her complaint. This was retaliatory, and as such, he was being investigated. This is what I assume led him to leave that institution and come northward to the hospital I worked at.

This, coupled with the emails I had saved and some recorded conversations, was enough for me to eventually come forward.

TAKEAWAYS

1. **Things will never change unless you change what you are doing:** True change happens only when you take action, even if it means confronting deeply ingrained systems of inequality. As I learned, waiting for fairness from others is futile. Real progress begins with the courage to speak out and demand better.
2. **Know your worth and stay only where you feel valued:** If your efforts and contributions are consistently undervalued, it's a sign to seek an environment that recognizes your worth. Staying in a place that devalues you is not loyalty; it's a compromise you don't have to make.

CHALLENGES TO YOU

1. **Take stock of your workplace culture:** Evaluate whether your organization's culture aligns with your values and supports your growth. Ask yourself, "Is this a place where I feel respected and valued?" If the answer is no, consider seeking opportunities elsewhere or advocating for systemic changes that promote equity.
2. **When something feels unfair, document it:** Keep a detailed record of incidents that illustrate discrimination or unequal treatment, including emails, meeting notes, and verbal exchanges. Make sure you save all documentation on an outside email account and computer. Your company email will be shut off and inaccessible to you once you leave your employment and can be looked through by your employers. This documentation can be invaluable when presenting your case to leadership, human resources, or external bodies.
3. **Understand your state's requirements to tape-record meetings:** Some states only require one person's consent, which can be you. Having audio to verify statements can validate your memories and incriminate those denying certain instances or comments.

Chapter 11

THE MURKY MIDDLE

"*More is lost by indecision than wrong decision. Indecision is the thief of opportunity. It will steal you blind.*"

—CICERO[80]

History is not kind to women who come forward and stand up for themselves against male harassment. Look at the hesitancy of rape victims, who fear they will be vilified in the media and in court if they come forward. In 2016, the EEOC (Equal Employment Opportunity Commission) found that "approximately 70 percent of individuals who experienced harassment never even talked with a supervisor, manager, or union representative about the harassing conduct."[81] EEOC stated that "common workplace-based responses by those who experience sex-based harassment are to avoid the harasser (33 percent to 75 percent); deny or downplay the gravity of the situation (54 percent to 73 percent); or attempt to ignore, forget or endure the behavior (44 percent to 70 percent)."[82] I did all these strategies. But none of them worked. I was called to my chair's office more times than I can remember. In 2003, Cortina and Magley reported in the *Journal of Occupational Health Psychology* that 66 percent of employees who reported harassment experienced subtle or overt retaliation.[83] This was my experience as well. They also note that harassment was especially prevalent in male-dominated fields. Because of all this, many workers just quit. I certainly started to contemplate quitting.

※ ※ ※

I knew years ago that I was in a toxic environment. But for some reason, I stayed. I stayed way too long.

I wanted to believe all the empty promises of "It's going to get better," "We'll fix it," and that the inequities "will be corrected in the next schedule."

But they weren't.

Nothing changed. Change is hard for a person and even harder for a group of people. Getting everyone to agree and buy into the need for change was impossible. Obviously, some benefited from the imbalance. They had no reason to want change. Change causes fear of the unknown, the unintended consequences. Change is scary!

In my heart, I knew I wanted to leave; I had to leave. But then my primitive brain, the one designed to keep me "safe," would begin to fire. It would pepper me with questions like "What are you going to do? Why give up your career? How will you pay for vacations? What will people think?"

All the questions designed to keep me "safe" kept me paralyzed. They kept me from action. They left me wanting a change but not deciding to do it. They left me with lots of indecision.

Indecision, though, is a decision.

It's a decision to stay stuck. To not move forward.

It kept me in the same circumstances, which were unhealthy

for me. Fear of making the wrong decision led me to make the decision to never decide.

It is there that is the "murky" middle, or as my high schooler would say, the "musty" middle. It's that area where you are stuck vacillating, ruminating. You can't see forward because of the fog, the gloom. Something murky is dim, gloomy, or hard to see through clearly. Think of the dark fog around a haunted house or the cloudy, muddy water in a swamp.

Musty is something that lacks originality and vitality. It is old, stale. Both murky and musty is how it feels to be stuck, wanting change but too afraid to act on it.

There is also the sunk cost fallacy. According to Oxford Languages, this term, popularized by Richard Thaler, is a phenomenon that describes how "a person is reluctant to abandon a strategy or course of action because they have invested heavily in it, even when it is clear that abandonment would be more beneficial."[84] It's a real, repeatable, and predictable psychological phenomenon that biases our informed decision-making in irrational ways. Examples of this phenomenon include staying to watch the remainder of a movie you find boring because you already paid for the ticket or keeping an article of clothing you never wear in your closet because it's expensive. A more extreme example of this is that people who climb Mount Everest often don't turn back in time because of just how far they have gone or because of all the months and years they have trained or prepared even though they know the risk of continuing when bad weather may kill them. The impact of the sunk cost fallacy can be not only distressing, but it can even be lethal in some circumstances.

I spent five extra years because of this. I was a partner. I had been there for over twenty-three years. I knew a lot of people and had created a reputation. It would take me "forever" to get here again if I were to leave. So I stayed.

My sunk cost fallacy led to my indecision, which became my default decision. Ruminating about things did not help. It delayed me from moving forward.

But then I remembered that if I wanted a change, I had to change what I was doing.

I needed to be the heroine of my own story and not wait for someone else to come fix it!

So I contacted a friend, a female surgeon, who had left our hospital a few years back. She had her own male toxic environment to deal with and eventually was fired, yet according to the hospital, she simply "did not have her contract renewed." Not being privy to all human resource matters but knowing she was one of the most talented surgeons, I was floored when she left. Here was a woman, highly trained, subspecialized, well known in her particular field, who was one of the hardest-working and more caring surgeons I had ever met. If one of her patients was in the ICU, she could be contacted at all hours to help or meet with family. She truly was one of a kind. I personally referred my sister to her when she needed a surgeon. Yet she was "let go" or "not renewed."

I had heard rumors that she'd filed a lawsuit for "wrongful termination" and had sued the hospital and won. I knew I needed help. I needed someone who had insight into how to navigate the legal waters I might have to tread into, despite wishing it had never come to this. So I reached out to her. She could not share the details of her settlement because of her non-disclosure agreement, but she said she would be happy, if I had her subpoenaed, to aid in my case as far as speaking about the male-dominated, toxic operating room environment. She also gave me the name of her lawyer who specialized in employment law. I called him. This was my next big step.

※ ※ ※

Without going into the nitty-gritty, let's just say that whoever said "the wheels of justice grind exceedingly slow" knew what they were talking about. Lodging an official complaint with the hospital about gender discrimination and harassment within my department was a burdensome decision, certainly not easily made. I had spent over two decades building a reputation within this hospital. I honestly couldn't believe it had come to this. I felt the full spectrum of emotions. I felt sad and heartbroken. I felt anger and disappointment that the "system" had "allowed" or enabled this to happen. I wanted to believe that those in power truly must not have known this was happening, especially in today's day and age, but then why was no one helping? Why was I met with a dead end whenever I sought help? I felt betrayed by my colleagues, hurt and shocked that they did not help me or the other women. I felt outraged that in 2021, women were still dealing with this. I felt scared. I knew this was not going to be easy. But deep down, I also knew it was the right thing to do. Not just for me but for all the women who didn't speak out. The women who might not have the same resources to hire a lawyer to fight the fight. For all the women who were gaslit into thinking it was their fault. I felt like I needed to do it for all the younger women, too, so it might not happen to them.

I have two daughters who are amazing, and I try to teach them that they can be anything they want. I want to believe that they will be met with a level playing field and will be judged and promoted based on their contributions and skill, not on their gender.

The decision to lodge a formal complaint was not made overnight. It took me over a year and a half after obtaining a lawyer to decide to file. In that time, I did a lot of soul-searching, working through all the above emotions. I also listened to podcasts on women's empowerment and found supportive Facebook groups for female physicians. I read a ton of books and focused a lot on personal growth.

I also found the world of coaching. I learned to extract thoughts from factual circumstances and learned that how I face events is in my power. Circumstances are just that: circumstances. It is our thoughts about the circumstances that create responses and feelings in us, which lead us to act and then generate our results. It was therefore within my power to control the narrative of how I responded to circumstances put before me. I gained my power back!

I was no longer going to be the victim of discrimination. My chair could choose to not compensate me the same as my male colleagues. He could choose to demote me and "fire" me from my committees. He could craft "manly man contests," and he could send inappropriate emails. He could state openly that women were not promoted because they chose to have children. Those were just some of the many facts and circumstances that I faced. I chose how to respond.

WHERE TRUST DIES, MISTRUST BLOOMS

My story is not a fairy tale, nor is it over.

Growth is painful. Change is painful. But nothing is as painful as staying stuck where you don't belong.

In 2018 I went to a conference in Boston with a few colleagues. One specific breakout session was about how to transform from the mindset of an employee to an engaged owner invested in outcomes. Employees show up and do the bare minimum. Engaged owners go beyond the minimum expected output and truly are in it to win it.

Per the session, three main elements need to be present to foster an "ownership" mindset:

1. An environment where you feel valued
2. An environment where you feel you can grow
3. Trust in leadership

Sounds simple, yet when we all reflected on this, we realized our current workplace lacked all three. We were widgets in a master spreadsheet, moved from location to location without any consideration for our areas of advanced training, interest, or expertise. We felt like we were just numbers and easily replaceable. We were individually not valued.

There was no interest in advancing opportunities for our education or professional growth. There was no yearly meeting asking us what our desires and hopes to advance were. There was no time given for our continuing education, unless we used our vacation time, no time for research to advance our careers, no time for lecture creation. We were just expected to churn through cases like an assembly line. One partner, somewhat callously, likened it to working at a warehouse where an employee is expected to just "keep loading the trucks." We were to take care of patients, one after another, and generate revenue.

Trust was long gone as well. There was no transparency

regarding call allocations, workloads, nonclinical time allocation, or resource distribution. Never mind daily release times.

We were a hot mess, and as much as people were clamoring for change, nothing seemed to.

Every year promises were made, but few were kept.

I knew this was not the place for me anymore. I was miserable. I was constantly frustrated by the lack of equity. I was frustrated by being passed over for advancements by inexperienced and younger male colleagues. I was frustrated and quite honestly sick of all the microaggressions, anti-female comments, and comments that were thrown around as if they were jokes. Deep down, when people make off-color jokes, they often believe some truth in them. There was no magical superhero who was going to come flying in and fix all these problems.

Yes, there's the saying that "the grass is always greener" elsewhere, but I was tired of standing on the scorched earth from our mismanagement. There were too many hurtful comments, too many disregarded pleas for fairness, and there was no trust. I needed a change.

Again, change is hard. Changes are painful, and growth can be painful too. But staying in a place where you don't belong? That's truly painful.

So I decided I needed to start crafting an exit plan. I needed to empower myself to move on and make things happen for myself. I had to find the solution I was looking for. I decided to take ultimate control and 100 percent responsibility for my happiness and for my career. I was no longer willing to sit in a situation in which I did not feel valued, I did not feel like I could grow, and I did not trust leadership. I wanted more.

I started listening to podcasts. I started reading as many books as possible. I started looking toward other women physicians who had been through what I'd been through, who'd endured years of frustration and put-downs from male colleagues. I looked at how they found different paths. I started to look at other successful people who had lives and who lived with elements that I wanted. I wanted control over my success. I wanted to control my life schedule. I was tired of being at the whim of a scheduler, at the whim of a spreadsheet that told me when and where I had to be. I wanted to be able to see my son run in a college track meet. I didn't want to have to plan everything a year and a half ahead of time, which is when we chose vacation for the following year. I looked toward people who had that kind of flexibility, and I tried to reverse engineer my life.

Once I started taking control of my life and I felt like there were opportunities ahead for me, I seemed to fret less about the day-to-day frustrations at work. I knew there was more coming. I was working toward a better future, and this positive energy created momentum within me. I was no longer sitting back ruminating on how I was a victim. I was going to overcome it. I was no longer waiting for a superhero to come in and fix things. I would be my own superhero. I was not relying on luck. I was going to create the future that I so desperately wanted.

TAKEAWAYS

1. **Change is hard but necessary to achieve different results:** Growth and change often come with discomfort, but staying in a situation that no longer serves you is far more painful. Embracing change is the first step toward crafting a better, more fulfilling future.
2. **To achieve different results, you must choose different options:** I said it in the last chapter, and I will say it again. Doing the same thing repeatedly while expecting a different outcome only keeps you stuck. To create meaningful change, you have to take deliberate action and make different choices.
3. **Find an ally:** Navigating toxic environments is challenging, but having an ally can provide critical support and guidance. Allies can share resources, offer insight, and help you see the possibilities ahead when you feel stuck. This person could be one of your role models or someone older who understands the place you're in. It could be a peer who's in a similar situation. Or it could even be a mentee or someone younger who can offer a fresh perspective and wants you to succeed.

CHALLENGES TO YOU

1. **Start small, but dream big:** Identify one small step you can take today to move toward a change you've been avoiding. It could be seeking advice, researching options, or even acknowledging your desire for something different.
2. **Indecision is a decision, so decide:** Reflect on a recent decision, and assess whether fear or indecision influenced your choice. How could you approach a similar situation differently in the future?
3. **Look outward for inspiration:** Reach out to someone who has faced similar challenges or achieved goals you aspire to. Learn from their experiences, and ask for advice or encouragement.

Chapter 12

VICTORY BUT WALKING WOUNDED

"The truth will set you free, but first it will piss you off!"
—GLORIA STEINEM[85]

"A fighter never gives up. His scars are his ornaments.

He may never be whole, but he's bigger than all his battles and beautiful, even in his brokenness."
—MONA SOORMA[86]

My future prospects in the group and at the hospital seemed nonexistent anymore. Unfortunately, my group supplied anesthesia services at almost all the surrounding hospitals and ambulatory centers in the state. I also had a noncompete that stated that I could not practice within a thirty-mile radius of any site our group worked at for two years after I left. This pretty much denied me from working in the state, at least without having to move or travel significantly.

I certainly was not about to uproot my family—my daughter, a high school junior, and my husband, who luckily had a thriving financial consulting business—all because I stood up against a male misogynist.

With the aid of my lawyer, I filed a complaint with the Equal Employment Opportunity Commission (EEOC), the federal agency that fights workplace discrimination in the United States. Outlining all that occurred to me with supporting documents and evidence once more was an emotionally exhausting task. Each time I relived the raw emotions that were exposed upon the initial insult.

Then there was the waiting game.

The EEOC had to evaluate my concerns and allow my group to respond. This had an obligatory thirty-day wait. Those thirty days were filled with second-guessing myself. I continuously wondered what they would conjure up about me. I knew they would try to paint me in a horrible light. They had to. But wondering what they would say or do was frightening. I knew they would go into attack mode.

I have left my position. I am no longer practicing medicine, my dream job since I was eight. I am no longer helping patients through their surgical adventures or attending to intensive care sick patients. I am no longer educating tomorrow's caregivers. I no longer receive a paycheck.

I tell myself I am on a hard-earned sabbatical, regrouping and waiting to see what is next. This is true. I am regrouping—licking my wounds, taking a deep breath, and reflecting on all that has happened.

Did I know it would come to this?

The answer is, full-heartedly, no. I wrongly assumed that once the chair's behaviors and how horribly I was treated were exposed, others would support me. I assumed the hospital would not only remove him, which they did, but that I would be reinstated to my positions. I thought this would "wake up" the institution to realize what happens on individual and system-wide levels. I assumed they could use my story as an example of what would not be tolerated. As the "diversity" banner waves brightly in the auditorium, and the DEI (diversity, equality, and inclusion) office continues to hire and espouse policies, I assumed this would be a rallying cry.

I also assumed when my colleagues, who I've known for years, heard rumors it was me, they would support me, reach out to me to see if I was OK, and work to quell the rumors.

I was so wrong.

SCARS OF VICTORY

A nine-month investigation ensued after I lodged my complaint. The investigation was difficult, as I had to recount all the events over and over again. Each time the scar burrowed a little deeper. I would sit across from colleagues I respected and share how I was belittled and stripped of hard-earned positions, how I had to dance around gendered comments, and overall how I felt victimized. I had to hope that they would understand the gravity of the situation, that they would not "blame me," as the victim is often blamed in similar scenarios. I also had to wonder who knew what was transpiring behind closed doors. What they were saying about me or plotting to do to me if this investigation found in the chair's favor. I felt so alone at work and confided in no one, as I did not know who I could trust. I also supplied a list of others who had witnessed the chair's behavior or who also had similar encounters with him. However, I was not privy to who they chose to interview, or, of course, what others said. I only hoped that each would speak the truth and share what experiences I knew they, too, had suffered.

At the conclusion of the investigation, the hospital decided to remove my chair from his position and title. I "won," so to speak; they believed me. This was not something that I, or others within the hospital community, had witnessed before. Shock and disbelief fell across the department. Unless you were specifically interviewed by the investigatory committee, you did not know an investigation was even occurring, so many had no idea what was going on. Details were not specifically shared, to keep my and his confidentiality. This was perhaps not necessarily in my best interest because for some who might have benefited from his tenure and might have been promoted or in his good graces, they were baffled that he could be dismissed. Rumors began to circulate.

"Do you know what happened to him?"

"I heard he was being himself and it upset a sensitive person."

"I heard someone was using this to promote her own professional career."

"He never did anything to me; he's a good guy."

Many wanted to fill in the story themselves. They wanted to postulate what had happened.

Certain individuals known for propagating gossip never wanted to look like they did not have the inside story, so they just made up a narrative that fit their purposes. This snowballed, and within twenty-four hours, the department rumor mill had named me as the sole complainer against their "beloved leader." I was vilified, and he was practically canonized. Even some women came to his defense because he never did anything to them, so he must not have done anything to me. The classic blame the victim. Disbelieve the woman.

An emergency departmental meeting was called for on a

Thursday morning, which was typically our grand rounds day. It was August, and I was on vacation, trying to distance myself from my unhappiness surrounding my work situation, but I decided to attend the meeting via Zoom. No specific agenda was announced, but I had hoped there would be a hospital representative to share what had happened and disclose why the chair was being removed. I had thought the hospital would want to take this opportunity to showcase how they took gender discrimination seriously and how it would not be tolerated. After all, within the auditorium are banners declaring some of the pillars on which the hospital prides itself: academics, patient-centered care, research for tomorrow, and diversity, equity, and inclusion.

Unfortunately, that was *not* what happened. There was no hospital representative, no hospital announcement. They let my chair craft an announcement of why he "chose" to step down. He literally stood before the department and all those on Zoom and stated that he and his wife decided he would step down for personal and family reasons. As if that was not bad enough, the hospital's chief medical officer sent a hospital-wide email within a few days announcing the chair's decision to step down and discussing how he had done great things for our department. It was all positive for him. There was *never* a statement of what really happened. No one except those who had been interviewed would have known this was a fabricated web of lies he was spinning.

When the truth is not told, people tend to fill in the gaps of a story with their own narrative that serves them. His allies, not knowing there was an investigation, not knowing the hospital interviewed upward of fifty people, not knowing all the emails he sent, recorded interactions caught on tape, and his history of gender discriminatory actions, came to his side.

Within two days, a petition was circulated by some women in leadership positions from within the department supporting him. It was specifically sent to the female members of the department and signed by numerous colleagues, both nurse anesthetists as well as physicians. This was truly unbelievable to me. The fact that people would sign a petition in support of someone without knowing all the facts behind why they were dismissed was unconscionable. Knowing that the hospital would not do this on a whim or they could be sued for wrongful termination did not dissuade people from blaming me. What was wrong with people? I honestly could not believe it. I was horrified. I was a pariah. I was no longer welcome. People would walk past me without making eye contact. People I had known for over twenty years, who I worked side by side with, people I had shared birthday celebrations with, shared milestones with, just ignored me. Whispers followed me. I no longer went to my office. I no longer ate with colleagues. I no longer fit in.

He, on the other hand, portrayed himself as the wronged individual. Again, he saw nothing wrong with his behavior. He never accepted that he did anything wrong. Never had to come to terms with the fact that you cannot pay women less than men for the same job. That you cannot state that gender discrimination is not a thing. That you cannot send emails with male genitalia on them. He still believes he did nothing wrong. My private practice group also stood by him. Happily passed him off to the hospital down the road, which we also had a contract with. I'm not sure how he passed the hospital credentialing board, which typically asks if you have ever been investigated for unprofessional behavior, but that's a different story.

Perhaps it was my overwhelming desire to be professional, to be a person of integrity, to "take the high road," or to not fall victim to the rumor mill by chiming in to this conversation. In truth, it was simply that I was uncomfortable with how to respond. Terms such as gender harassment, sexual assault, intimidation, bullying, and retaliation are definable on paper but remain elusive when applied to human behavior. How does one prove the motive of these questions? Can I prove they were retaliatory, aimed to make me uncomfortable, or were they mere human nature grappling with an unusual occurrence? Prove intonation. Prove "sensitive" equates to misogyny.

I felt his allies had already turned their guns on me. They started to target me and looked for "payback," as I had taken out their beloved leader. After all, some of them had benefited from his leadership tenure. Some women had been promoted. It was not as though he maltreated all women. If you were willing to look the other way, laugh at his inappropriate jokes, and have your name associated with his emails with sexist and ageist comments, then you were seen as one of the inner circle.

So I said nothing. I acted as if something urgent was awaiting my attention and politely left conversations. I walked around in silence, never sharing my side of the story. I left all the assumptions out there unanswered. It seemed that his side of the story, as he told it, was the only narrative. No one heard the real story. But why should I suffer this experience in silence? Silence is another form of subjugation. The sad truth is that his patriarchal and misogynistic behavior violated the physician code of conduct, and instead of lasting accountability, he was quietly ushered from one hospital system to another. He was protected—financially, professionally, reputationally, legally.

It turned out that his being stripped of his chair position led him to be 50 percent unemployed. He then was able to "moonlight" on the days he was no longer chair and, by doing so, doubled his income that year. It was as if he won the lottery!

By contrast, the accuser, me, was ostracized and marginalized. I never went back to my shared office space within the department. I found remote computers to perform my charting. I ate alone in the cafeteria. I was woefully alone. Unsure who I could trust given all that had happened. So I talked with no one. After working at a place for twenty-four years, I was alone.

※ ※ ※

After my chair was removed, or "allowed" to resign, the executive team of my private practice group seemed to circle the proverbial wagons around him. They did not seem interested in finding out the truth. They immediately called a meeting where our governing body of physician colleagues voiced their unanimous support of him as a leader and physician. This was quickly followed by the executive management team also stating they fully supported him. Oh, but by the way, they were going to have an "independent" investigator look into it. She was hired by the practice, reported findings to the executive team only, and could speak only to those employed by the private group. So no outside physicians, nurses, or OR staff could be interviewed who might corroborate allegations. Nor was talking with her mandatory. Only those who wanted to chat with her did. Needless to say, a few months later, another supportive email came from our executive management team stating that the majority of individuals interviewed stated they had not experienced discrimination. One can see how this form of "investigation" of course led to the outcome the admin team wanted. So basically, he was left in the group, in good standing, with the full support of our physician management team as well as executive management. He was honored at resident graduation, his photo gracing our internal email newsletter. He was one of about 5 percent of the staff invited to join the residents on their retreat, which also included a free day off of clinical responsibility, while the rest of us worked.

I honestly couldn't believe it, but then again, I could. The male privilege that had a stranglehold on our group ever since I arrived was enough to allow him to avoid full responsibility for his actions. Despite an outside nine-month investigation finding him guilty of gender discrimination, our group still embraced him. And I, although never officially named, was the evil one. I was the one stripped of all my leadership positions, marginalized to work at outside ambulatory centers, ostracized, and shunned.

THE FALLOUT AND FORCED DEPARTURE

Needless to say, although I was vindicated by my chair's removal, which many see as a huge win, the victory was not without cost. I cried many tears, had countless sleepless nights, and fell into a depression that required therapy and pharmacologic intervention. It has cost me friendships, as watching your "friends" initially not help you when you need it but also seeing them treat you as a persona non grata is heart-wrenching. It's cost over $100,000 at this point, with over four years of legal fees.

It also cost me my job, as I could no longer stay in a place that was so toxic to me personally. I was a wreck. I felt like my professional life was out of control because, in many aspects, it was. I was stripped of all leadership positions I had worked for years to attain. I was no longer a person people sought advice from. I was on the outside. I turned to food, one thing I could control, I suppose, and unfortunately gained thirty pounds. Before the chair's removal, I was walking on eggshells and wondering what he would do to me next. I had to relive the humiliating accounts numerous times as I was called to be interviewed throughout the institute's investigation, as well as during the investigation by their committee concerning his retaliation. Numerous hours of retelling the incidents of abuse and thus being revictimized by the process of those leading the investigation.

The crazy thing was that despite all that I was going through, I was still attached to the comfort of what I knew, my career I had built. It was familiar. The thought of leaving that behind filled me with fear of the unknown. My gut was telling me to move forward, but fear was telling me to hold on. My primitive brain, ever protecting me and placing survival as the number one priority, wanted me to stay and interjected thoughts that made me feel crazy. I needed to choose which voice to follow: the one encouraging me to leave the safe harbor or the one holding me back.

The logical, limiting voice never went away completely, but I chose to amplify the voice that trusted my ability to move forward. For the sake of my mental and physical health, I could not stay working at my company or walking the same halls as people who perpetuated or excused toxic discriminatory behavior. So on St. Patrick's Day 2023, I channeled the luck of the Irish and gave my six-month notice.

WOULD I DO IT ALL AGAIN?

I am scarred from this experience. I feel like I am the poster child for the term "walking wounded." I wonder, if I could do it over again, would I do it differently? My answer is no. I know my response was appropriate. I know that his behavior was meant to diminish me and keep me in my "place." I want a different environment for all women, especially those who have their whole careers ahead of them. I see my two daughters, and I think of them. I want better for them. I want opportunities and workplaces free of gendered expectations and limitations. Free of good old boys clubs and patriarchy. I also want a different playbook. I want the victims to be armed with the opportunity to share their side of the story, and to be emboldened. I want the perpetrator to be the one left shamed. I want to be able to share my story. I want to be heard.

I know the victims deserve that. I want his actions to be broadcast throughout the institution and the medical community at large. I want his behavior to be reported to those in charge of his medical licensing. I want him not to be merely passed to the next unsuspecting hospital and for his behavior to have to be withstood again. I do not want other women to have to hear him state how there are not that many women leaders because they choose to take themselves out by having babies. I do not want other women to have to bear witness to his outdated, patriarchal thinking and actions and to have to create a folder on their laptop of all his communications laced with microaggressions. I do not want them to have to mentally anguish over hiring a lawyer and withstand years of investigations and strategy sessions.

It's too much. Why do women need to have to prove that he cannot behave professionally? At one of my interviews during the investigation stage, I was told that I seemed more evolved when it came to these issues. They asked me if I thought he could be educated and if he would change. My answer was an emphatic no. He would never change. He already had done similar misogynistic behaviors at another institution before applying to ours. But the "process" shielded under human resources did not expose his true reasons for fleeing his prior place of employment, and thus he just left. That is how I was exposed to him. He clearly did not learn his lesson from the prior hospital. He merely shifted northward and traumatized the next cohort of unsuspecting women. He did not seem to learn his lesson then, so why should I expect a different outcome this time? The shielded HR files protect him. He will move on to another hospital, which is what has happened.

SYSTEMIC PERPETUATION OF TOXIC WORKPLACES

The outcome of my legal battle remains uncertain and will likely be concealed by an NDA (nondisclosure agreement). This is emblematic of a broader issue in healthcare, where insulated harassers and ineffectual leaders thrive. Those in power are shielded from the consequences of inappropriate behavior, perpetuating and amplifying existing power differentials.

NDAs are commonly presented as tools to protect all parties (including victims), but in practice, they disproportionately benefit perpetrators. Organizations often use them to protect their own reputations and shield sensitive information from public exposure. Employers may justify NDAs as a way to ensure privacy and confidentiality during or after a legal settlement, but their primary function is usually to limit legal and reputational risk for the company—not to safeguard victims. While an NDA could, in theory, offer certain protections to victims (e.g., shielding them from public scrutiny or defamation), this is more of a secondary effect than an intentional design feature. NDAs frequently prevent victims from discussing their experiences publicly, which can create isolation and prevent systemic change. Moreover, NDAs often allow perpetrators to avoid accountability and transparency, perpetuating harm.

Under the terms of the NDA, the perpetrator of gender harassment is not required to disclose why he was removed from his role. He is free to spin his departure as a personal decision or frame it around familial obligations rather than being held accountable for his actions. This is what happened in my case. Even worse, this lack of transparency enabled him to secure another position at a nearby hospital and, later, as a per diem employee—earning more than he did under his previous contract. Despite being removed from his chair position, he continued working in the same physician group, portraying himself as a victim of persecution while I was ostracized. This outcome emboldens perpetrators, teaching them they can escape consequences and even benefit financially from the system's shortcomings.

This experience leads me to argue that NDAs must be reformed to protect victims or taken out of settlements altogether. Coworkers and teams have a right to know if someone was fired for sexual or gender harassment. Clear communication—whether through meetings or emails—about the reason for a perpetrator's termination would send a strong message that such behavior is taken seriously and won't be tolerated. Moreover, future employers should be informed of a perpetrator's past misconduct, allowing them to make informed decisions about hiring and assessing the risk such an individual poses to their workplace. Transparency like this is essential for transforming workplace culture and holding harassers accountable.

This idea isn't new. After witnessing firsthand how perpetrators are shielded, I began researching what others are doing to address this systemic issue. Organizations like Lift Our Voices, a nonprofit co-founded by Gretchen Carlson and Julie Roginsky, are leading the charge.[87] According to their data, 60 percent of US workers have experienced or witnessed workplace discrimination, and 40 percent reported retaliation after speaking up. They highlight how "toxic behavior happens at work →

survivors are bound by their contracts from talking about it," pointing to NDAs as a key mechanism that silences victims and enables systemic issues to persist. Victims who come forward are ten times more likely to face attrition than to receive financial compensation or emotional support. To address this, Lift Our Voices advocates for eliminating forced arbitration and NDAs that protect perpetrators, aiming to foster transparency and accountability.

In recent years, two legislative acts have also contributed significantly to this goal: the Ending Forced Arbitration of Sexual Assault and Sexual Harassment Act (EEFA), which went into effect in March 2022, and the Speak Out Act, enacted in December 2022.[88] The EEFA prohibits employers from requiring workers to settle sexual assault and harassment claims through arbitration, ensuring victims can take their cases to court. The Speak Out Act limits the enforceability of pre-dispute NDAs in cases of sexual harassment or assault, allowing survivors to share their stories publicly if they choose. These acts represent important steps toward dismantling the systemic protections that shield perpetrators, though there remains much work to be done to fully realize the acts' potential.

Healthcare systems have an opportunity—and an obligation—to reform policies that protect victims, provide clear investigative guidance for leadership, and establish meaningful penalties for perpetrators. These changes are critical as more women enter the medical profession, only to leave far earlier than their male counterparts. We already face physician shortages and underserved communities across the country. We cannot afford to lose talented women to outdated systems that fail to protect them.

The medical field is at the threshold of a much-needed cultural revolution. By fostering transparency and accountability, we can ensure the existence of workplaces where harassment is neither tolerated nor excused. It's time to act decisively and end sexual harassment in medicine once and for all.

TAKEAWAYS

1. **The road to victory is long and nonlinear:** The process is far from straightforward. Filing a case isn't a magic solution. It requires extensive evidence-gathering, external meetings, financial resources, and a significant toll on mental energy. Even after overcoming one obstacle, new challenges and misogynists (including other women) arise. Yet despite the difficulty, the journey is worth it because I loved my job as a doctor, and I have a newfound respect for myself after fighting for what I believe in.
2. **Fighting for yourself builds respect for yourself:** Standing up for what you believe in, even when the odds feel insurmountable, cultivates self-respect and empowers you to challenge unjust systems. If you feel like you're being selfish and you can just endure the current system, remember you owe it to younger people following in your footsteps to make the workplace a better place for them.
3. **NDAs silence change; speaking up creates it:** NDAs are designed to maintain the status quo. They prioritize protecting companies, shielding perpetrators, silencing victims, and perpetuating toxic workplace cultures. We must reject systems that place corporate reputations and profits above the safety and well-being of individuals. Silence allows harm to persist. Change begins when we refuse to stay quiet. So tell your story and change the culture at your workplace.

CHALLENGES TO YOU

1. Check to see if you have an NDA in your work contract. If so, is it still enforceable in your state?
2. Research where your elected legislators stand on the issue of NDAs. Reach out to your legislators to start a conversation to eradicate NDAs from toxic workplace issues.
3. Subscribe to the Lift Our Voices newsletter to stay informed and find opportunities to help change workplace cultures and mechanisms that perpetuate toxic environments.

Chapter 13

RECALIBRATION, REDIRECTION, AND REDEFINITION

"When nothing is sure, everything is possible."
—MARGARET DRABBLE[89]

September 17, 2023, I was free. It was a weird day. I technically didn't even work that day. It was a Sunday, and I had vacation the previous week, planned months before I even put in my six-month notice. What that meant was that my actual last day of work was September 10, a day that passed with no particular fanfare. I had attended many retirement parties for partners on their last days over the years, even performing a parody of a song for one of my best friend colleagues, but there was no such event for my departure. Not that I needed a cupcake or fake small talk from my partners who had spent the past few months ignoring me in the hallways. But a simple "thank you for twenty-four years of work" or a small gathering of those in other departments who didn't have a vendetta against me would have been welcome.

All of a sudden I was free. I no longer worked fifty-to-ninety-hour weeks. I no longer had one weekend every month "on call." I no longer had to pull all-nighters. I could attend my kids' track meets and parent-teacher conferences. I could sit on the couch and watch Netflix well into the night without having to worry about a 5:15 alarm. I could eat lunch with my husband on a weekday. I could take a spontaneous quick trip with my daughter to Montreal during her winter break (not advised—too cold). I could walk my dog during the sunny parts of the day. I could even get another dog. I had so much freedom! Sometimes it's about the little things. I had time to enjoy and live life again.

I had gained time. I had gained control of my schedule for the first time in my adult life. But most importantly, I had gained respect for myself. I always knew I could do hard things. For one, I had gained acceptance to one of the hardest medical schools to get into and had graduated with an MD degree. I had survived a grueling internship, residency, and fellowships. I could do hard things. But this was something even bigger. This I did for the greater good. I didn't have to take this on. But I did. I could have just gone along with the status quo. I could have just shut up and played the game. I could have let him get away with it and let all the good old boys get away with it, but I didn't.

First, I needed to learn how to be still.

Today there is so much emphasis on being busy. We rush from one task to another. Endless to-do lists with boxes waiting to be checked off. I am the queen of making lists. It actually was a joke at my rehearsal dinner and made it onto my engagement quilt designed by my bridesmaids. In our society, we wear our busyness as a badge of honor somehow. But why? Is it a part of our desire to not be seen as "lazy," to prove our worthiness, especially as women?

Research shows that when the brain is not actively focused on a task, it processes experiences, consolidates memories, and fosters innovative thinking through something neuroscientists call the "default mode network," or the DMN.[90] This means that stillness, daydreaming, and quite literally "doing nothing" benefits us in ways often overlooked. It's in these moments of idleness and reflection that some of our best thinking happens, why people go on walks to clear their minds or have "aha moments" in the shower. As someone who was constantly working and running from one thing to the next, I often didn't make time for this essential process to happen. My first step toward self-care was letting go of the expectation to constantly be "doing something" and giving myself this gift of stillness to reflect, to discover new hobbies and passions, to find who I am (as cheesy as that sounds).

Sometimes when filling out a form, you're asked what your hobbies are. I always resented this question when I came across it. Seriously, hobbies? As if anyone had time for those. But deeper down, I realized I felt ridiculous when asked this question because I never knew how to answer it. Is it possible that after over fifty years, I didn't have a single hobby? Other people I knew were busy playing tennis, crocheting, painting, and gardening. You name it. It seemed like everyone else had a hobby.

Is it wrong to write that my kids were my hobby? All my spare time, all the time I wasn't at work, I wanted to be with my kids. I wanted to go to their games. I wanted to meet with their teachers. They filled in any of my time gaps. But now, I had three in college, and one in high school so busy with her academics, athletics, and social calendar that she had no time for me. So I started to focus more on myself.

I filled my days with the things I like to do, which I still hesitate to call "hobbies." I took long relaxing baths. I played lots of Rummikub and Skip-Bo. I walked my dogs (yes, I actually got that second dog, taking him in off Facebook). I did my "research," which consisted of getting lost down various rabbit holes of Google, such as my kids' track competitions or possible vacation destinations. I played "spot the difference" games and completed word searches. As silly as this sounds, these activities were essential in the sense that they helped me reclaim my time as *mine*. I did all these things for me.

But amid all this, each day I found myself wondering what it was I was meant to *do*.

One of the scariest parts about the possibility of leaving that kept me in place for so long, even when I was clearly unhappy, was giving up on my five-year-old self's dream of being a doctor. It was this dream that had dictated my entire life. It informed which classes I took in high school, where I went to college, what cities I lived in, what activities I pursued in my spare time, which relationships I put effort into. I didn't mind it. As a matter of fact, I loved it.

But who was I if I wasn't a doctor? I didn't know.

So after I had quit and had caught up on a few weeks of sleep and doing absolutely nothing, I did some reflecting. What parts of being a doctor did I enjoy? It certainly wasn't the sleep schedule. Some people do it for the money or the prestige, and that's fine, but those were never my motives. Some people loved the fields of anatomy and pharmacology, and while I enjoyed studying these, they were more of a means to an end. With time, I came to realize why I loved being a doctor: I loved being there to help patients in their greatest times of need.

I truly felt a calling to medicine and was blessed that people I barely knew, and only met briefly preoperatively, trusted me at their most vulnerable times. They trusted me to put them to sleep and to make sure they stayed that way until the time to awaken. They trusted me to alleviate their pain, to be present at their most vulnerable times and at their most joyous times, the births of their babies. They allowed me to care for their dying loved ones in the intensive care units, to help them gently leave this world to go to the next. I had the privilege of helping train the next generation of physicians, working with med school students as well as high school students who were contemplating medicine as a distant career. One sticks out in my mind. I followed his journey from high school student to fellowship-boarded ophthalmologist, as well as a husband and father.

Figuring out *why* I loved being a doctor was a big step in figuring out how to move forward now "post–being a doctor," if there was ever such a thing. My new question that drove me was: How can I spend my time in a way that will help others and give me similar feelings of fulfillment?

The answer to that question comes with a lot of trial and error. Previous to my exit, I became certified as a Botox injector, thinking I could give women some newfound confidence. If there was one thing I knew how to do after twenty-four years of anesthesia, it was giving injections! I also had become a certified professional life coach, thinking about how I could help people take meaningful action to craft the outcomes they want. If I could change my life, I could certainly help others change theirs with activities to help them open their minds to be perceptive to change, visualize alternatives, and be empowered to take steps forward. I took classes on women's empowerment and joined groups of other women physicians on social media to build solidarity.

In these groups, I have gained clarity on how important it is to stand for what you believe in. I have learned how we are all socialized into believing certain gender constructs are "normal." I have learned how to empower myself against these gender-limiting constructs, and I want to raise awareness so that others can understand how limiting these beliefs can be. I have gained a new passion for helping educate as many as possible on the subject and awakening others to it. This is what led me to want to share my story and write this book in an effort to help other women feel less alone in their experiences with misogyny and inspire change in the medical system.

I wrote this book to help other women in the medical field and in male-dominated fields at large, but that is certainly not the extent of my audience. I also want men to read my book. I want this to just be the start of the conversation surrounding gender in the workplace.

I have never thought of myself as a writer. As my daughter comically put as my update in our holiday card this year, "Despite not having taken a writing class since twelfth grade, Kolleen is now writing a book!" I may not be a writer, but I do like to think of myself as a change-maker. I have these experiences. I have a voice. And I have a duty to help others still in the medical system. Through this book, I have found my new purpose of helping others and feeling fulfillment in my work.

TAKEAWAYS

1. **Don't be afraid of recalibrating, redirecting, and redefining!:** Many people associate changing course with giving up or failing, but in reality, it takes great strength to reassess and shift direction. Whether it's a career pivot, a lifestyle change, or simply a renewed perspective, recalibrating allows for growth. Studies show that people who embrace change with a learning mindset are more resilient and adaptable, leading to greater long-term satisfaction in both work and personal life. Instead of seeing transitions as setbacks, view them as opportunities to redefine what success means to you.

2. **It's necessary to be still and "do nothing":** Society often glorifies busyness as a sign of productivity and worth, but neuroscience reveals that taking breaks and allowing for stillness actually enhances creativity, memory consolidation, and overall well-being. The brain's default mode network (DMN) activates during periods of rest, helping to process past experiences, strengthen problem-solving skills, and generate creative ideas. Stillness isn't about doing nothing—it's about allowing your mind the space to function at its best.

3. **Purpose evolves over time:** Many of us tie our identity to our profession or past goals, but purpose is not a fixed destination—it evolves. What once fulfilled you may no longer resonate, and that's OK. Research on career satisfaction suggests that people who regularly reassess their values and align their work with their deeper purpose experience greater well-being and motivation. Instead of holding onto a path that no longer serves you, give yourself permission to explore what truly excites and fulfills you now.

CHALLENGES TO YOU

1. **Practice doing nothing:** Block out at least ten to fifteen minutes each day for intentional stillness—whether it's sitting in silence, taking a slow walk, or simply staring out the window without distractions. Pay attention to how it affects your mood, focus, and creativity. If you feel restless at first, that's normal! Over time, you may start to notice increased clarity, better decision-making, and even unexpected insights about your next steps in life.
2. **Rediscover joy and curiosity:** Think back to childhood. What activities made you lose track of time? Was it painting, writing, exploring nature, or storytelling? Choose one activity that sparks curiosity or joy, and commit to trying it without any pressure to be "good" at it. Notice how it makes you feel and whether it reignites a sense of passion or fulfillment. Hobbies are not about productivity; they're about connection to yourself.
3. **Invest in yourself:** This one goes hand in hand with the previous challenge. Take time for you. Pursuing hobbies, self-care, or passions isn't selfish—it's a critical step toward becoming your best self. When you thrive personally, you bring greater energy and joy to your relationships and work. So whether it's a hobby, self-care activity, or any other random time-fillers, indulge!
4. **Reflect on what is important to you:** Why did you get into the work that you currently do? What is most important to you in your job? What are you most proud of in life? If your current job no longer meets your needs or you don't feel valued, feel free to take your talents elsewhere. Inform your next step in life based on these answers so that you can continue to find meaning and excitement in your next steps in life. Feel free to use the guide I put together to help you in your reflection.

REFLECTION ON WHAT IS IMPORTANT TO YOU

Reflecting on your current role

- Why did you choose your current career path? Was it for personal passion, financial stability, or external expectations?
- What aspects of your job bring you the most joy or fulfillment? Which tasks or interactions do you look forward to most?
- When was the last time you felt proud or accomplished at work? What made that moment significant?
- How do you feel about the balance between your personal and professional life? Does your work align with your values and priorities?
- Are there parts of your job that drain your energy or feel misaligned with your goals or interests?

Exploring what matters most

- What personal values are most important to you (e.g., creativity, security, connection, autonomy)? How does your current work align with these values?
- Who or what in your life inspires you to keep going, even during challenging times? How can you prioritize those sources of inspiration more often?
- What are the nonnegotiable aspects of a fulfilling life or career for you? (e.g., flexibility, recognition, meaningful impact)
- Beyond work, what activities or experiences bring you the most happiness or peace?

Envisioning the future

- If your current job is no longer meeting your needs, what are three potential alternatives that excite you? What steps could you take to explore them further?
- What legacy or impact do you hope to leave behind, either in your career or personal life?
- If fear or external expectations weren't factors, what would you pursue next in life?
- Looking ahead five or ten years, what does your ideal day-to-day life look like? What can you do now to move toward that vision?

Taking action

- What is one small change you can make today to align your life or career more closely with your values and passions?
- Who can you reach out to for support, advice, or mentorship as you consider your next steps?
- How will you measure success in this next chapter of your life? What metrics matter most to you: financial, emotional, or relational?

Chapter 14

WOMAN VERSUS WOMAN

"Be the woman who fixes another woman's crown, without telling the world that it was crooked."

—ANONYMOUS

One of the most unexpected aspects of this ordeal was how many female physicians, nurses, and colleagues defended the perpetrator, spreading gossip and circulating petitions on his behalf rather than pausing to consider what it might be like to be in my position as the victim. Where was the solidarity? Didn't they realize they didn't have the full story? Shouldn't they, as women, understand what it feels like to be on the receiving end of misogynistic behavior? Even if they hadn't experienced his comments personally, couldn't they have thought, *Hmm, this sounds serious; maybe I should check in with those affected before jumping to conclusions?* Or at the very least, they could have taken a passive stance and let things be. Instead, they actively chose to defend the male perpetrator and turn their backs on a fellow physician, and a hurt woman at that.

At different points in my career, I wondered why women did not seem to help other women as much as I thought they would have. There seemed to be almost aggression between female physicians or female staff and female physicians, much more so than between male and female physicians or staff and male physicians. It seemed that often when a female physician achieved something, other women were jealous instead of happy for her.

In a 2023 article by Mary Henderson, "Identifying and Mitigating Aggressive Behavior Among Female Physicians," she reported on results that Dr. Gokli and others had found when looking at female-to-female aggression in the medical field. Dr. Gokli revealed a troubling trend: The majority of respondents admitted to witnessing female-to-female aggression in the workplace, with nearly half (47 percent) saying they had experienced it firsthand. Even more surprising, 36 percent confessed to engaging in this behavior themselves.[91] The impact is undeniable: 39 percent reported that it created significant stress and tension, while 46 percent of women on the receiving end said it directly altered the course of their career. The ripple effect of this dynamic on women's professional lives is profound.

Dr. Gokli explained that jealousy, insecurity, and personality clashes were cited as the main causes of female-to-female aggression. Both men and women hesitated to report this behavior due to fears of retaliation or being seen as problematic. She suggested that this aggression stems from gender inequality, noting that women in male-dominated fields often internalize gender bias and apply the same stereotypes to their female subordinates.

I believe part of this aggression or jealousy comes from a "scarcity mindset." Medicine is a world where men are at the top of the food chain. There are extremely few women. Occasionally, there may be one woman on a board or in leadership. The American Hospital Association's 2022 National Health Care Governance Survey Report—a triennial poll that had more than nine hundred hospital and health system respondents—found the percentage of female board members had increased from 30 percent in 2018 to 36 percent in 2022.[92] When you are acclimated to seeing only one woman in an organization "succeed," it becomes a contest; if she succeeds, you won't. This scarcity mindset breeds competition, where you have to take out the other women or you will never rise up.

This mindset isn't unprecedented. In school, we are taught that there can be only one homecoming queen, one or two soccer captains, one female lead in the school play. This competition mindset is perpetuated within work culture, and especially with tokenization, it can be true that only one woman gets promoted. As of 2023, only 10.4 percent of CEOs running Fortune 500 companies were women.[93] The same year, women comprised only 11.8 percent of the roughly fifteen thousand C-suite roles that were assessed.[94] This makes female leadership and success look rare and perhaps makes us feel like there is not much space for women. We see that there are simply fewer jobs and opportunities for women and that we need to fight other women for them. This creates hostile, unsupportive relationships among female colleagues.

Again, concerns about tokenism crop up. *Perhaps they won't hire or promote me if they promote another woman.* The idea that two women may be on the board is unthinkable because it is not typically seen. This creates cognitive dissonance. So many women see all other women as competition. We tend to believe that there is room for only one.

Here's the secret, though: There is more than enough room

for one. Ruth Bader Ginsburg's response to questions about female representation perfectly encapsulates her fearless challenge to the status quo. Her answer is quintessentially RBG (and anti-scarcity mindset!): "And when I'm sometimes asked when will there be enough [women on the Supreme Court]? And I say when there are nine, people are shocked. But there'd been nine men, and nobody's ever raised a question about that."[95]

Female physicians, all women, need to abandon this scarcity mindset where we feel as though only one woman can make it to the top. Understanding that there is room for more than one will eliminate the constant competition and instead allow alliances to form, whereby women can help each other attain higher goals.

Here's a simple fact: We live in a patriarchy—a world designed by men, for men, where masculine qualities and figures are valued as the standard of leadership. This shapes our models of authority, success, and even behavior.

For women, living in this system often means internalizing societal biases against themselves and other women. This internalized misogyny can show up in subtle but telling ways: A woman might distance herself from traditionally feminine things, like avoiding pink because it's "girly" or judging other women more harshly for their choices, from makeup to clothing. It can lead to scrutinizing other women's behaviors without holding men to the same standards. This mindset even leads women to doubt the competence of other women, especially in leadership roles.

At its core, internalized misogyny is the absorption of societal beliefs and norms that undervalue women, ultimately leading women to unconsciously project those beliefs onto themselves and others. Living in a patriarchal society means that women, like men, are often exposed to negative messages about femininity and women's abilities. These ingrained messages can lead to women unconsciously devaluing their own gender and, in turn, projecting that negativity onto other women.

In professional environments, particularly male-dominated fields like medicine, this internalized bias can be even more pronounced. When women compete for limited leadership opportunities or struggle to achieve recognition in spaces historically dominated by men, internalized misogyny can cause them to view each other as competitors rather than collaborators. This mindset may explain some of the female-on-female aggression observed in the medical field. Instead of supporting one another, women may undermine or sabotage their female colleagues, fearing that only one of them can succeed in spaces where female representation is scarce.

When women internalize these societal biases, they may adopt the same behaviors they have faced from men. For example, women in senior positions may hold their female subordinates to higher standards or dismiss them as being too emotional, lacking leadership qualities, or needing to "toughen up." This isn't because they consciously believe women are lesser but because they have internalized the same misogynistic structures that prioritize masculine traits over feminine ones. In the medical field, this can lead to harsher treatment of female peers, where women doctors feel pressured to be more assertive or cutthroat to "prove" their worth in a male-dominated space. As a result, female physicians may find themselves isolated and unsupported, not just by male colleagues but by their female peers as well.

The antidote to internalized misogyny lies in recognizing it for what it is: a learned behavior rooted in systemic inequality. Women in medicine, like in all professions, need to embrace each other's strengths and talents rather than viewing each other as competition. By uplifting and supporting one another, women can not only combat internalized biases but also pave the way for a more inclusive and equitable work environment.

We can't help that these thoughts of internalized misogyny are sometimes our first thoughts. But we can control our second thoughts. And we can reframe our mindsets. Instead of scoffing at women who love to wear high heels or who have perfected their cat eye, why don't we appreciate their confidence and style? We need to stop seeing femininity as a weakness and instead see it as a strength.

So how do we do this? There's this theory called amplification or the "shine theory."[96] This theory champions collaboration instead of competition and can be especially useful when applied to women interacting with one another. Coined by *Call Your Girlfriend* podcast cohosts Aminatou Sow and Ann Friedman, the shine theory can be applied to help women shine a light on other women instead of tearing them down.[97] It's about building deep, intentional support systems. It's about advocating for each other, celebrating each other's victories, and supporting each other in trying times. It champions building confidence to reduce insecurities and feelings associated with a scarcity mindset.

TAKEAWAYS

1. **Women are not the enemy; scarcity is the problem:** Female competition in medicine is often rooted in the false belief that there's room for only one woman at the top. The scarcity mindset creates unnecessary rivalries and fosters an environment where women undermine instead of uplift

one another. In reality, when one woman succeeds, she paves the way for others. Recognizing that gender equity benefits all women can help shift the focus from competition to collaboration.

2. **Internalized misogyny is a learned behavior—and it can be unlearned:** Women, like men, are conditioned by societal messages that devalue femininity and female leadership. This can manifest as holding female colleagues to higher standards, doubting their abilities, or failing to support them in moments of need. Acknowledging these biases is the first step toward dismantling them. By consciously choosing to amplify other women's voices rather than diminish them, we can break the cycle of internalized sexism.

3. **Amplification and support build stronger workplaces:** Studies show that women in male-dominated fields experience more workplace hostility from other women than they do from men. This stems from systemic barriers that pit women against one another. However, research also indicates that when women actively support, mentor, and advocate for each other, they are more likely to reach leadership roles and positively impact institutional policies. Fostering an environment where women encourage one another leads to better career outcomes for all.

4. **Women physicians face unique barriers and need allies:** The challenges women face in medicine—being overlooked for leadership, experiencing "hepeating," or being judged more harshly—are not just individual struggles; they are systemic problems. It is crucial to create strong female alliances in the workplace to counteract these biases. Women who stand together and advocate for each other create real change in the medical field.

5. **Femininity and strength are not opposites:** Women in medicine should not feel pressured to downplay their femininity to gain respect. Internalized misogyny often leads to the belief that femininity is weak, but traits such as empathy, emotional intelligence, and collaboration are strengths, not liabilities. Reframing these qualities as powerful, rather than as obstacles, can help shift workplace culture.

CHALLENGES TO YOU

1. **Complete the internalized sexism inventory:** Take a moment to reflect on the inventory provided at the end of this chapter. Identify any biases you may unconsciously hold, and consider where they may have originated. Challenge yourself to shift these thought patterns by actively supporting and advocating for women in your workplace.
2. **Challenge gender stereotypes in medicine:** If you hear a female colleague being described as "too emotional" or "not assertive enough," push back. Ask, "Would we describe a male colleague the same way?" If you notice a woman being interrupted or dismissed, support her by redirecting attention back to her. Encourage open conversations about gender biases with both male and female colleagues.
3. **Uplift female voices:** Practice amplification in the workplace. Mentor young women. Value historically marginalized voices, and take their suggestions seriously.

INTERNALIZED SEXISM INVENTORY

PERCEPTIONS OF COMPETENCE & TRUST

- Do I instinctively perceive male physicians as more competent than female physicians?
- When selecting a personal physician, do I assume a male doctor will be more experienced or skilled?
- Do I unconsciously expect female colleagues to "prove" their competence more than I do male colleagues?
- If I were undergoing a high-risk surgery, would I feel more confident if the surgeon were a man?
- Have I ever reassured a patient who seemed doubtful about a female doctor's skills by emphasizing her credentials in a way I wouldn't for a male doctor?

PROFESSIONAL RELATIONSHIPS & SUPPORT

- Have I ever found myself feeling competitive toward a female colleague in a way I wouldn't feel toward a male colleague?
- Do I hesitate to advocate for another woman's promotion or leadership position because I worry it will reduce my own opportunities?
- Have I ever dismissed or minimized a female colleague's complaint about sexism in medicine?
- Do I give more weight to the approval or mentorship of male senior physicians than female ones?
- When in a leadership role, do I hold female subordinates to higher standards than male subordinates?

WORKPLACE CULTURE & BEHAVIOR

- Have I ever doubted or second-guessed myself in a meeting, even when I knew I was right?
- Do I hesitate to speak up in meetings unless I feel 100% prepared, while male colleagues confidently voice ideas with less caution?
- Have I ever had my idea ignored, only to have it validated when restated by a male colleague?
- Have I ever unconsciously allowed male colleagues to interrupt me more than female colleagues?
- Have I ever chosen not to correct someone who mistook me for a nurse or an administrator rather than a physician?

APPEARANCE, BEHAVIOR & SELF-PERCEPTION

- Do I feel pressure to conform to a certain appearance standard (e.g., wearing makeup, styling my hair a certain way) to be taken seriously as a doctor?
- Have I ever worried that being too assertive in a professional setting would make me seem unlikable?
- Do I adjust my tone, body language, or phrasing to seem less "intimidating" when speaking to male colleagues?
- Have I ever minimized my own success by attributing it to luck rather than my skills and hard work?
- Do I feel the need to apologize excessively in professional settings, even when it's unnecessary?

INTERNALIZED SEXISM INVENTORY cont.

LEADERSHIP & REPRESENTATION

- When reviewing applicants for a position, do I find myself more critical of female candidates' qualifications than male candidates'?
- Have I ever doubted whether a female colleague was "tough enough" for a leadership role?
- Do I assume that female doctors with children are less committed to their careers than their male counterparts?
- Have I hesitated to take on leadership roles myself, fearing I would be judged more harshly than a male counterpart?
- Do I assume that women doctors in administrative roles are there because they couldn't "hack it" in clinical work?

PATIENT CARE & BIAS IN MEDICINE

- Have I ever assumed that a female patient's symptoms were exaggerated while taking a male patient's symptoms more seriously?
- Do I ever unconsciously treat male patients with more clinical authority and female patients with more emotional reassurance?
- Have I ever second-guessed a female colleague's clinical judgment in a way I wouldn't with a male colleague?
- Have I witnessed patients preferring male physicians for procedures and felt unsure about how to address it?
- Have I ever hesitated to challenge a male colleague's incorrect diagnosis or medical decision, even when I knew I was right?

Source: Karrie Keyes, "Challenging Internalized Sexism," *SoundGirls* (blog), accessed June 13, 2025.

Chapter 15

TAKE UP SPACE AND USE YOUR VOICE

"It took me quite a long time to develop a voice and now that I have it, I am not going to be silent."

—MADELEINE ALBRIGHT[98]

As COO (clinical operating officer) for five years, I was responsible for ensuring staffing levels and appropriate subspecialists at sites, covering call slots when vacated for sickness or other emergencies, and any number of other operational issues. Keeping the engines running was the goal.

I worked tirelessly, while not receiving my nonclinical days off as described in the job description, and as needed. I did it on my own time or, realistically, at the expense of time with my family. Those immediately in my shared office space and close friends knew how much I did. I never tooted my own horn; I just got it done.

When our new chair came, he was getting to meet everyone. At the same time, there was an opening for a new position in the

OR. The ideal candidate for the job of OR director was someone who had expert-level knowledge of the inner workings of the operating rooms: capacity, OR size, case complexity, surgical block needs, and how to shuffle cases from room to room efficiently and fairly. They also had to know people—relationships matter! I was interested. But as a typical woman, at the time, I was hoping someone would acknowledge me and ask me rather than coming forward myself. *Huge* mistake.

No one will have your back better than you do.

Recall a study I referenced earlier in Chapter 6: Men apply for a job when they meet only 60 percent of the qualifications, but women apply only if they meet 100 percent of the qualifications.[99] The finding comes from a Hewlett-Packard internal report and has been quoted in *Lean In*, *The Confidence Code*, and dozens of articles. It's usually invoked as evidence that women need more confidence. As one *Forbes* article put it, "Men are confident about their ability at 60%, but women don't feel confident until they've checked off each item on the list."[100] The advice: Women need to have more faith in themselves.

One day, my chair came to our shared office space where two of my colleagues and I were. He began to ask who he might consider for the position of OR director. My partner stated clearly, "You're looking at her." He went on to espouse all that I have done and my knowledge of the operating rooms, how I kept our company afloat the last few years, how I was well liked and respected, and how I had proved myself over the years. This was echoed by my other partner.

However, to my surprise, nothing came of it.

The following Thursday, at grand rounds, my chair went on

to extoll the attributes of a male colleague and all he had done to warrant the position. Don't get me wrong; this man is a great clinician and respected. But he was never in leadership, was never on our governing body, and did not organize or run the operating rooms as much as I did. He was not as experienced. But he had the one needed characteristic, which I did not have: the Y chromosome.

He eventually was offered the job and accepted it.

If only I had listened to my mother. She was a strong advocate of putting yourself out there. "You'll never know unless you try"—ergo, my acceptance to Columbia University College of Physicians and Surgeons.

Who knows if I would have been chosen. I'll never know.

And again, I love the Wayne Gretzky quote: "You miss 100 percent of the shots you don't take." Well, I missed that one. And it hurt!

Somewhere along my indoctrination into the medical arena, I lost my confidence and voice. I felt like I didn't belong. I felt like my voice, my opinion, was not as valid as others' in the room. I was in a practice heavily dominated by men. I was in the 10 percent of the people in my anesthesia group who did not benefit from being born male. I did not have the overconfidence that comes from being in the majority. I either voluntarily stifled my own voice or found myself on the receiving end of being interrupted or "hepeated." At times I muted myself. I didn't want to speak up for fear of reprisal. I didn't want to seem like a "know-it-all" or be called a whiner if drawing attention to an issue. Women, myself included, mute themselves.

My voice, if I did dare to speak, would be silenced, talked

over, and disregarded. A 2014 study from George Washington University revealed that men interrupted women 33 percent more frequently than they did other men.[101] Men interrupted their female conversational partners 2.1 times during a three-minute conversation. That number dropped to 1.8 when they spoke to other men. The women in the study rarely interrupted their male counterparts—an average of once in a three-minute dialogue.[102]

Besides being interrupted, often my ideas were not acknowledged or they were repeated by male colleagues. This male colleague then was met with great acknowledgment and acceptance of the idea he commandeered as his own. This is called "hepeating." Hepeating is defined as "when a man appropriates your comments or ideas and then is praised for them being his own."[103] "Hepeating" is a concept many women are probably familiar with, according to *Business Insider*'s Lindsay Dodgson back in 2017. This is not to be confused with "mansplaining," which is when a man condescendingly explains something to you, or "manterrupting," when he literally talks over you. All contribute to toxic environments, which lead to silencing women.

For me, it felt as though I was constantly ignored, interrupted, or "hepeated." One particular meeting comes to mind. I was in a crowded hotel ballroom at a business meeting. I would guess approximately sixty or more people were there, including partners, partners-to-be, and administration. I knew what I wanted to say, but before speaking, rehearsed it in my head. I wanted it to land right. I was worried; I didn't want to look "stupid" by voicing my opinion. I finally raised my hand and spoke up. After it was over, nothing. No one seconded it or tacked on to what I said. After about two minutes, another partner basically reiterated exactly what I had said, and then as usual, others chimed in, "I agree with him." I was so annoyed. I stated to the two sitting near me that basically the last speaker agreed with me because if he agreed with the man who copied what I said, he agreed with me. It's the transitive property: If a = b and b = c, then a = c.

Later that evening, I was in the women's bathroom with the head of our human resources department. I mentioned to her how frustrated I was that Dr. Joe Blow stated exactly what I'd said and was acknowledged, whereas no one responded when I stated the same thing prior. Her response: "Well, what do you expect? You're in a room full of men."

I was outraged inside. It was nice that she acknowledged the situation, but perhaps I'd expect my HR lead to correct it—to fix it! Not just acknowledge it as a de facto irreversible truth that I would have to live with forever.

The problem is my voice, our voices, matter. Studies have shown that patients taken care of by women have lower readmission rates. Companies with a woman as CEO or on their board perform better. Committees with women on them solve problems better.[104]

So I learned over time that the best way to be heard is to speak. Speak with confidence and authority. It starts with commanding space. When I say that, I mean start by sitting at the table. Often women will sit on the periphery, sit in the back. Start by sitting in the front of the room. Sit up straight with shoulders back. I'm not a posture fanatic, but what I mean is do not cave in. Do not sit low in the chair; rather, take up space.

I often remind myself before entering the room that I want to be front and center. You have to be in it to win it. You have to be seen to be called on and it is easier to be seen and heard if you are front and center. Try power posing before going into the room. Stop by the bathroom, and replicate the iconic Wonder

Woman power pose. This expansive body posture includes standing upright, legs shoulder-width apart, and hands on your hips with your thumbs facing backward and other fingers facing your navel. This will energize you and give you confidence. Talking in front of a group can be hard. When I started my position as COO at my practice it meant talking at our practice management meeting in front of approximately fifty or so people every month.

I used to get very nervous and almost had to rehearse what to say. The more I did it, the easier it became. I also realized that the adage "practice makes perfect" somewhat applies. Practice does make it less scary and perhaps a more polished experience, but in no way should you worry that it has to be perfect. We are human, and perfection is not necessarily the desired result. No one can be perfect, but we all can and should be perfectly comfortable owning our own space! Owning our voice and using it to engage in the conversation is essential.

TAKEAWAYS

1. **Your voice is your power—use it:** Too often, women wait to be recognized for their work rather than stepping forward and asserting their value. This reluctance to self-advocate is deeply ingrained but must be unlearned. Studies show that men apply for jobs when they meet only 60 percent of qualifications, whereas women feel they need to meet 100 percent. The lesson? Speak up. Apply for the role. Take credit for your ideas. Your voice is your power, and you deserve to be heard.
2. **The workplace is not a meritocracy—visibility matters:** Hard work alone is not enough. While it may be comforting to believe that merit alone will get you ahead, the reality is that those who are vocal, visible, and self-promoting are often the ones who are recognized. Women disproportionately assume that their work will "speak for itself," but research suggests that women are more likely to be overlooked for promotions unless they self-advocate. Sitting at the table—both figuratively and literally—is crucial to be seen as a leader.
3. **Confidence is built through action, not perfection:** Confidence doesn't come from waiting until you feel 100 percent ready; it comes from doing. The more I spoke in front of groups, the easier it became. Many women hold themselves back due to perfectionism, fearing they will say the wrong thing or appear inadequate. But confidence grows through repetition and experience. Take action before you feel completely prepared—you'll be amazed at how much you already know.

CHALLENGES TO YOU

1. **Apply for something outside your comfort zone:** Think of a leadership role, project, or promotion that interests you, even if you feel underqualified. Write down why you are qualified. Take the first step toward applying, whether it's reaching out to a mentor, submitting your name, or practicing your pitch.
2. **Own your physical presence:** Do this in multiple ways. Before an important meeting or presentation, try power posing for two minutes in a private space. Notice how you feel afterward. In your next meeting, consciously sit at the table instead of the periphery. Speak with intention—no qualifiers like "just" or "I think." State your ideas with confidence.

Chapter 16

THE BIG PICTURE

"Gender equality not only liberates women but also men from prescribed gender stereotypes."

—EMMA WATSON[105]

Obviously, the issue of gender inequity matters to me as a woman and as a doctor. But it matters to me, too, because I am a mother, a wife, a sister, a daughter, and an aunt. There are a lot of people I care about who do or will need healthcare sometime in their lives, and I fear that the system is broken and is losing so many great physicians.

Women now make up more than 50 percent of incoming medical school classes.[106]

However, women also retire from medicine at earlier stages.[107] There was an amazingly talented resident I helped train who went on and did extra training in a cardiac anesthesia fellowship. After thirteen years of post–high school education and training, she finally became an attending. One day, she approached me, looking quite hesitant but clearly with something on her mind. She was married, had two young children, and confided in me that she was overwhelmed. She did not think medicine, her job, would be like it was after all her training, and she point-blank asked me how I stayed in it for so long. She was thinking of quitting it all. I couldn't believe it. This was a woman in her prime. She'd just finished her years of training, and she was already thinking of leaving it all behind. The medical field cannot afford to lose women like her. But the reality is, we are.

Research shows that over 20–40 percent of women physicians go part-time or leave medicine in six years after completing their residencies, compared to 3.6 percent of men.[108] If women are more than 50 percent of the medical school classes and statistically are eight times more likely to leave the practice within six years, that will mean far fewer physicians caring for us.

Recently I tried to make an appointment to see my doctor. The wait time was six months. I also tried to see a specialist, a dermatologist. The wait time was greater than nine months. My daughter was transitioning from a pediatrician to a general internist. She called the same office my husband and I were in and was told they were not accepting any new patients. At another practice, it would take over ten months to see a doctor. The United States already has a physician shortage, and in some states, especially in rural areas, the shortage is frightening. By the year 2034, some studies project a shortage of between 37,800 and 124,000 physicians in the United States.[109] If women continue to drop out of practicing, that shortage will be exponentially larger.[110]

WOMEN'S TOUCH IN MEDICINE: LOWER MORTALITY, MORBIDITY, AND REMISSION RATES AND INCREASED HOLISTIC CARE

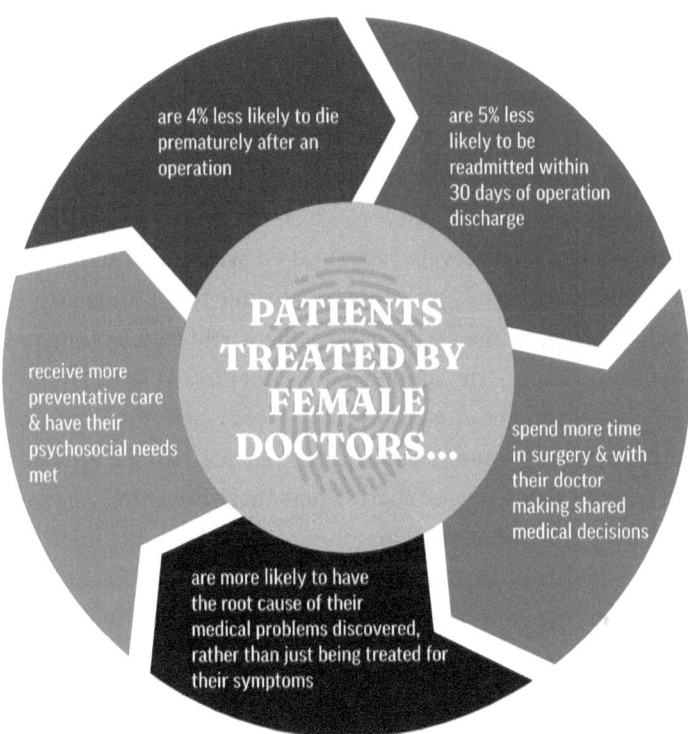

Besides the pure number of physicians the system will lose, it will also lose some of the best providers. Women physicians have lower morbidity and mortality scores and lower readmission rates, and women physicians spend more time with patients and provide more preventative care.[111] For instance, one study published in *JAMA Internal Medicine* revealed that patients treated by female physicians had a 4 percent lower chance of dying prematurely and were 5 percent less likely to be readmitted within thirty days of discharge.[112] This higher quality of care is partly attributed to female physicians spending more time with patients, adhering more strictly to clinical guidelines, and incorporating more preventative care practices.[113] Moreover, female doctors are more likely to offer psychosocial counseling, which is essential for addressing the emotional needs of patients and promoting long-term health outcomes.

Female patients, in particular, saw the most meaningful improvements. Male doctors are more likely to underestimate women's pain levels, heart and GI symptoms, and stroke risk.[114] Researchers suggest this may be due to multiple factors, including a potential for more empathetic and patient-centered communication styles among female doctors, which is particularly beneficial for women, who are more often misdiagnosed or have their symptoms minimized.[115] Hence, women are often more likely to feel at ease sharing personal or sensitive information with female doctors. This increased comfort can lead to the disclosure of critical details that contribute to a more accurate diagnosis and tailored treatment plan, ultimately improving the quality of care.

Let's examine a study that looks at the impact of gender dynamics in medicine, focusing on surgical outcomes. A 2021 study conducted in Ontario, Canada, analyzed over 1.3 million patients who underwent one of twenty-one common surgical procedures between 2007 and 2019.[116] The findings were striking: Female patients treated by male surgeons were significantly more likely to experience adverse postoperative outcomes—including death, readmission, or complications—compared to female patients treated by female surgeons. In fact, the adjusted odds of adverse outcomes were 1.15 percent higher for female patients with male surgeons.

Conversely, male patients treated by female surgeons fared no worse than those treated by male surgeons. This discrepancy highlights the nuanced and often gendered nature of surgeon-patient interactions. While the exact mechanisms behind these outcomes remain unclear, the study suggests that sex discordance in the surgeon-patient relationship can have tangible effects on patient health.

Here's another example. A study conducted in Florida between 2016 and 2019 tracked the health outcomes of patients over sixty-five receiving Medicare.[117] Among nearly 800,000 patients, the study found that 8.15 percent of women treated by female physicians died within thirty days, compared to 8.36 percent of women treated by male physicians. While the difference may seem small, it's statistically significant—closing this gap would save approximately five thousand women's lives each year. Interestingly, the study found no similar difference in male patients' outcomes based on the gender of their physician.

However, that doesn't mean that men don't feel the difference of the gender of their doctor. I came across one article written by a man who recounted why he prefers to be treated by a female physician. In the *Los Angeles Times*, he said:

> After seeing a series of male doctors who were not listening to me, in a hurry to get out of the exam room or appearing only mildly interested in figuring out the cause of my problem, I made the switch—and I'm not going back. While I found that male doctors typically decided what my diagnosis was and how to treat it before entering the exam room, female doctors tended to be open-minded about what my medical issues were and—gasp!—listen to my answers to their questions.[118]

He speculated that male physicians have a higher propensity to be driven by their egos. I agree with this statement. Women are more likely to double-check their work, spend more time on a problem, and take into account all facets of information. It's in these instances that I believe being judged by our gender is actually beneficial—we have this extra chip on our shoulders to prove ourselves and feel like we can't mess up, which allows us to deliver better care to our patients. The small silver lining to the dark cloud of misogyny!

This disparity in outcomes is not limited to the United States. Studies from countries like Sweden and Canada reveal that patients undergoing surgery with female surgeons similarly report better postoperative outcomes.[119] In the US, heart attack survival rates are higher for women treated by female physicians, highlighting how gender concordance between patient and doctor can play a critical role in emergency and intensive care.[120] These practices not only improve the quality of care but also contribute to a sense of safety, reducing the chances of complications or oversights. We need them personally as individuals and collectively to help the overall health of our society.

EMPOWERMENT BEYOND GENDER: HOW MEN BENEFIT WHEN WOMEN SUCCEED

When women gain more empowerment and representation in medicine, it is not just women who benefit—male physicians and men in society at large stand to gain too. Acknowledging and dismantling gender stereotypes creates space for more compassionate, flexible, and authentic expressions of identity, benefiting everyone.

Men traditionally face societal expectations to remain stoic, assume the role of sole provider, and avoid vulnerability, and these stereotypes can be stifling. This is commonly known as "toxic masculinity," and it can be emotionally and physically detrimental. For example, let's say a male doctor's parent just died. After taking the allocated time off work to attend the funeral and spend time with family, he returns to work but struggles to perform at his usual capacity. His male boss is unsympathetic and tells him, "Get over it already. You're a doctor, not some emotional wreck. Patients need you to man up and focus." This dismissive attitude not only trivializes grief but also reinforces the toxic belief that emotional expression is a sign of weakness, pressuring men to suppress their feelings and prioritize productivity over personal well-being. Such behavior creates a work culture that stigmatizes vulnerability and perpetuates burnout among all employees.

In the medical field, where emotional resilience and compassion are crucial, these norms can hinder men from showing vulnerability or building supportive connections with patients and colleagues. Male physicians might feel pressured to work without showing fatigue, spend less time with patients, or avoid asking for help, which can lead to burnout and decreased job satisfaction. All these factors negatively affect the care provided to their patients.

Outside of medicine, rigid stereotypes limit men who wish to pursue nontraditional roles, such as becoming stay-at-home dads or primary caregivers. Social expectations often undermine these choices, making it difficult for men to feel validated or empowered.

Research indicates that the emotional suppression many men exhibit has real costs: Men generally have shorter lifespans than women and are statistically four times more likely to die from suicide.[121] These disparities are exacerbated by a reluctance to seek help, partly due to societal pressures to "tough it out" alone.

Yet as women break barriers and create more balanced workplace environments, men gain the freedom to explore different expressions of masculinity and form deeper emotional connections. There is less tolerance for toxic masculinity and a culture of repressing emotions and not asking for help. When men stand alongside women to acknowledge and combat gender stereotypes, they help to create a system that values empathy, collaboration, and well-being. This empowerment ultimately benefits patient care, professional relationships, and the personal lives of both men and women alike.

TAKEAWAYS

1. **Women physicians are more likely to leave doctoring:** Despite making up over 50 percent of medical school classes, women physicians leave or go part-time at significantly higher rates than men. Research shows that 20-40 percent of women physicians leave medicine or reduce their hours within six years of completing their residency, compared to only 3.6 percent of men. This has profound implications for the future of healthcare, as physician shortages are expected to worsen, making access to quality care even more difficult. Addressing the systemic issues that push women out—such as workplace inflexibility, lack of support, and gender bias—is essential to retaining talented doctors.

2. **Gender equity in medicine benefits everyone:** Gender equity isn't just about fairness—it has measurable benefits for both patients and doctors. Patients treated by female physicians have lower mortality and readmission rates, and female doctors are more likely to follow evidence-based clinical guidelines, provide preventive care, and spend more time listening to patients. Moreover, research shows that male patients also benefit from female physicians, as they are more likely to receive patient-centered care and thorough evaluations.[122] Creating a more gender-equitable system isn't just about helping women; it enhances the overall quality of care and improves patient outcomes for all.[123]

3. **Women's voices in medicine improve patient safety:** Studies reveal that female surgeons have better postoperative outcomes, particularly when treating female patients.[124] However, these benefits are often overlooked due to deeply ingrained biases. In settings where women's voices are ignored or undermined, patient care can suffer. Encouraging diversity in medical leadership and ensuring that women's perspectives are valued can lead to more holistic, effective care models that ultimately improve health outcomes for everyone.

4. **Breaking gender norms benefits men too:** The push for gender equality in medicine doesn't just liberate women; it also allows men to redefine

their roles in the workplace and at home. Traditional expectations that men must be stoic, always in control, and career-focused can contribute to higher burnout rates, reluctance to seek help, and poorer mental health outcomes for male physicians. When gender norms are dismantled, men gain the freedom to practice medicine in a more compassionate, balanced way without fear of judgment.

CHALLENGES TO YOU

1. **Challenge gender stereotypes:** How do you personally challenge traditional gender stereotypes in your practice or in your home life? Men may feel societal pressure to suppress emotions and work without showing vulnerability. Reflect on how embracing a more balanced approach—where emotional resilience, empathy, and collaboration are valued—can improve your well-being, your relationships, and the quality of care you provide. Furthermore, reflect on how rigid gender norms may contribute to burnout, particularly for male physicians. Are there ways to embrace a more flexible, empathetic approach that encourages collaboration, vulnerability, and open communication with your colleagues? How can fostering a healthier work-life balance reduce burnout and improve your overall job satisfaction?

2. **Practice patient-centered care:** Given that research shows female physicians tend to spend more time with patients and incorporate more preventive care, how can you ensure that your practice fosters a more patient-centered approach, regardless of your gender? Think about how you might prioritize listening to your patients more attentively and offering holistic care that addresses not only physical symptoms but also emotional and psychological needs.

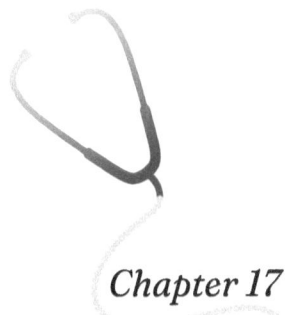

Chapter 17

LESSONS LEARNED AND MOVING FORWARD

"*The silencing of one woman is the silencing of all women. The awakening of women is the awakening of the whole world.*"

—DR. TERERAI TRENT[125]

What was the point of all of this? Of this book, of sharing my experiences, of living through all of this?

I started writing the book and felt empowered and at peace because I was putting the control back into my own hands. For so long, I was stifled. I was bullied and walking on eggshells. My daily work life was controlled by others—which assignments I had, which cases, and who I worked with. Which hospital or ambulatory surgical center I worked at, when I was released to go home, when I was assigned call. I had no control.

My committees, my leadership roles all had been stripped from me.

My voice had been silenced.

A lot of people talk about hitting rock bottom before a catharsis. I was at my rock bottom. I knew I had to make a change, and I had to speak up. Simply walking away was not in my DNA. With my identity as a conscientious, well-respected leader unraveling, I started asking myself those questions that seem to surface only when you're at your absolute lowest point: Who am I, and what do I really want?

The whole experience ignited in me a newfound purpose. I wanted to help embolden women. I deliberately choose the word *embolden* over *empower* because I truly believe we all already have the power within us. We just need the courage to use it.

I wanted to openly discuss the challenges unique to women in male-dominated spaces like medicine. I wanted to help continue a conversation about gender equity in workspaces and how to achieve it. I desperately wanted to help younger women who are just venturing out into the work world, like my oldest daughter is.

I wanted to take my power back and not be the victim but to make proverbial lemonade out of the very sour lemons handed to me. I wanted something good to come from all my torment. Without the past five years, without the demotions, the embarrassments, the harassing meetings, I may have never ended up writing this book and following my true passion.

WHAT I'VE LEARNED FROM THIS

What I've learned is that you always have the power to change. If you truly want change in your life, it starts with altering what you are doing. And to change your actions, you first need to change your thoughts. Shifting your mindset is the key to transforming your reality.

Along the way, you must rely on yourself. True loved ones will be there to lean on, but when times get tough, some "friends" may not stick around. You'll learn who really supports you, and that's OK. Trust in your own strength.

Remember, there is more to life than a job. Time is precious, and it shouldn't be wasted being unhappy or stuck in a situation that drains you. There's no such thing as failure—only lessons that teach you what doesn't work. Embrace uncertainty because it means that endless possibilities lie ahead.

Existing power structures are hard to change because powerful people must give up some of that power and go into the unknown. That's why I think the future of women at work will come from the current trend of female entrepreneurs leaving their current jobs in large numbers and creating their own enterprises. Those leaving corporate America, especially during COVID-19, did so often to find more meaning from their work. They wanted to find more fulfilling roles, to follow their passion projects, and they judged their current positions less on salary and monetary basis but more so on the intangibles: ability to grow, collaborate, feel fulfilled.

It has become more important for work to be meaningful. Empowering women to take ownership of their jobs and happiness and focus on what they can control puts pressure on the system, and it has to lead to change. But that won't happen until we stop mistaking empathy for weakness and realize that female success shouldn't hinge on us being more like men.

We need to accept that our institutions in the corporate world were designed by men with their worldview. Lots of incentives, rewards, and structures cater to that worldview.

Fewer women at the top is a clear signal that the system is dysfunctional, and it not only results in a lack of diversity but also crushes creativity and makes organizations slow or unable to adapt.[126] So women need to define success on their own terms. My recommendation is to orient the idea of success around well-being. I want to be a catalyst to embolden women in a way that harnesses the power they already have.

※ ※ ※

The traditional advice for women facing gender inequality in the workplace was to "grow thick skin" and tolerate the discrimination. This evolved into the notion of "fixing yourself," suggesting that women needed to change to fit into male-dominated spaces. Women were encouraged to adopt more masculine traits, such as assertiveness and competitiveness, and to integrate into male-dominated networks by hanging out with the boys. This mindset promoted the idea that women could succeed by beating men at their own game rather than challenging the systemic barriers and changing the rules to create a more inclusive workplace.

At the end of the day, we need to change the system that promotes masculine ideals and protects male perpetrators. To do this, we need to attack this challenge at both the individual level to change workplace culture as well as the institutional level to provide the structure for lasting change. I've put together some action items for each.

ACTION ITEMS FOR INDIVIDUALS

1. Look at yourself critically and think about how you are perpetuating gender stereotypes. Are you buying only your

daughters dolls and only your sons tools? How are you writing letters of recommendation for women versus men?
2. You need to start having more conversations. You need to talk to your peers, your colleagues, your supervisors, your family members, and your neighbors. You need to invite everyone to start thinking about gender roles and stereotypes and how we need to change the gender-normative expectations that society places on ourselves and each other.
3. Make the unconscious conscious by speaking up when you see gender inequity. This includes but isn't limited to men addressing comments only to men even when a woman asked the question, men interrupting women, and men introducing women by first name.
4. You need to understand the scarcity mindset and realize that we are not all in competition with each other. And especially understand that women are not necessarily competing with other women. If one person succeeds, that doesn't mean the other one will automatically fail. You need to change that perspective so that women can band together and work to amplify each other and lift each other up.
5. You need to support those who are bravely coming forward with issues regarding gender inequality. You need to stop disbelieving the victim, or worse yet, blaming the victim. Just because it didn't happen to you does not mean it didn't happen.

ACTION ITEMS FOR INSTITUTIONS
1. EDUCATION

Prioritize ongoing education around inclusivity and gender equity. This should include training programs that raise awareness about unconscious biases, the nuances of discrimination, and the importance of creating an inclusive work environment. A workforce educated on these topics is better equipped to foster supportive relationships and recognize problematic behaviors.

2. CULTURAL CHANGE

Effect a cultural shift within organizations to establish an intolerance for harassment, discrimination, and toxic masculinity. This cultural transformation is vital to create a safe and supportive environment for all employees. Empowering everyone to have a voice allows for broader ideas and has been shown to lead to more successful organizations.

3. ELIMINATE RETALIATION

Create safe reporting mechanisms for harassment or discrimination that do not put the reporter at risk of retaliation. These channels should be anonymous and non-biased, ideally situated outside of the human resources department, which may prioritize the organization's interests over individual employee concerns. Providing safe avenues for reporting is essential for encouraging employees to speak up about their experiences.

4. HR REPORTING SYSTEMS

Develop clearer HR and reporting systems. Individuals need clear HR systems through which they can report observations and experiences of sexual harassment. Processes to reduce risks of retaliation or gossip also need to be in place to reduce the fear of reporting. The Society for Human Resource Management recommends:

A. Having clear definitions of what constitutes harassment.
B. Including examples of prohibited conduct.
C. Explaining how victims and viewers of harassment should respond to and report harassment.
D. Outlining how HR should handle the process.
E. Expressing what disciplinary measures should be followed. Importantly, all complaints should be treated as confidential.
F. Protecting all employees against retaliation.

5. LEGAL ASSISTANCE

Make funding and support available for those who are fighting discrimination lawsuits. The prohibitive costs associated with hiring a lawyer can deter many women from coming forward. Expecting marginalized groups to be able to take on employers who have much deeper pockets is untenable. Resource limitations disable most from pursuing action against companies and corporations that are not abiding by antidiscrimination laws. By providing resources for legal assistance, organizations can empower their staff to advocate for themselves without the burden of financial stress.

6. PUBLIC ACCOUNTABILITY

Require companies to publicly report how much money they spend yearly fighting discrimination lawsuits and how much they have had to pay to victims. This would give employees and potential employees an idea of the culture at an organization. It also would decrease the stigma that you are alone if you are a victim and help victims realize that others also have faced issues with the same employer. Isolation is one reason you continuously second-guess yourself. You feel all alone. *I'm the only one, so maybe it really didn't happen or isn't that bad.* Gaslighting is effective in an environment of isolation.

7. TRANSPARENT SYSTEMS FOR HIRING AND PROMOTION

Foster transparency about the criteria for promotion advancement opportunities. Organizations need to hire based on skills and accomplishments rather than "fit."

8. INDIVIDUAL ACCOUNTABILITY WITH CONSEQUENCES

Hold accountable those who violate policies against harassment and discrimination. Establishing clear consequences for inappropriate behavior helps to create a culture of respect and reinforces the organization's commitment to maintaining a safe workplace.

9. REPARATIONS FOR SURVIVORS

Make reparations to anyone affected by perpetrators of discrimination or harassment. This includes offering support, resources, or career assistance to those who have been harmed.

10. NDAS

Revamp nondisclosure agreements (NDAs). NDAs are often included as part of the mandatory human resources forms that new hires must sign, and they bind over one-third of the US workforce. These NDAs often prevent victims from sharing their experiences and thus keep the perpetrator free from others knowing what occurred. Everyone should know what happened and what havoc and illegal activities an individual did to another.

As I previously mentioned, in December 2022 Congress passed the Speak Out Act which restores the voice of victims of sexual discrimination and harassment. In the "findings" section of the Act, Congress noted that approximately 81 percent of women and 43 percent of men have experienced some form of sexual harassment or assault in their lifetimes. The Act recognizes that "although more than one in three women have faced sexual harassment in the workplace, approximately 90 percent of alleged victims never file a complaint." Congress attributed "pervasive" sexual harassment and assault in the United States in part to the prevalence of nondisclosure and non-disparagement clauses in employment agreements.

The law will allow employees to talk about their experiences with harassment or assault at work by invalidating NDAs that force workers to remain silent. Although the Speak Out Act made headlines at the beginning of 2023, its practical implications for employers may be somewhat limited. Employers may still include nondisclosure and non-disparagement provisions in separation or settlement agreements executed after alleged incidents of sexual harassment or assault occur, subject to state or local law. NDAs need to end so that victims are not isolated and so that perpetrators are more accountable for their actions.

11. BOARD OF LICENSURE—MANDATORY REPORTING

Require mandatory reporting to the board of licensure for physicians found to engage in discriminatory or harassing behavior. Reporting to a professional database would ensure that these individuals cannot simply move to another institution without consequences.

Our current system depends on self-reporting. When a physician is applying for credentials at a new place of employment, they are asked whether they have been a subject of an investigation related to unprofessional conduct or if they have ever had their credentials revoked from a prior hospital. Typically, answering yes to this question would require further documentation as well as a possible investigation from the credentialing or licensing committee prior to allowing that physician to work at an institution or in the state. Currently, there is no mandatory hospital reporting to state boards when they undertake an investigation or if they find that a provider behaved unprofessionally. The investigation and findings are "hidden" under human resource documents and kept internal to that one hospital.

If a perpetrator is convinced that they do not participate in gender-biased behavior, even if found guilty of such by an outside investigation, I am convinced they will *not* self-report. Institutions are also complicit in that they "allow" perpetrators to resign before they are officially "fired." In that case, a person found guilty of unprofessional and discriminatory behavior is "allowed" to resign, thereby circumventing him from being stripped of his chair position of the department, and the hospital no longer has to relinquish his privileges. If they had, that would be reportable. But by his "choosing to resign," none of the reporting comes into play, allowing him to move on to the next hospital. Passing providers from one institution to another, hiding their behavior from credentialing and licensing bodies so that they can continue to perpetrate this behavior, is abhorrent.

※ ※ ※

Individual and institutional change are equally critical in reshaping our work culture and fostering gender equity. On the individual level, each of us can challenge the biases we carry and the stereotypes we unknowingly perpetuate. By creating more supportive, open environments where conversations about gender roles and stereotypes can thrive, we can help women feel more comfortable and empowered in their workplaces. When individuals speak up, support one another, and break free from the scarcity mindset, they contribute to a culture where women feel valued and heard.

However, true systemic change—change that reshapes the structures of power and dismantles institutionalized discrimination—requires more than individual actions. People leave when they don't feel valued. Look at me! Institutions need to foster environments that are intolerant of harassment, discrimination, and toxic masculinity. Real progress will come from altering the policies, practices, and accountability mechanisms that allow inequality to persist. Individual change plants the seeds, but institutional change is what will uproot the systems that reinforce gender inequality on a larger scale.

※ ※ ※

As we come to a close, I'd like to offer some advice for women in the workplace.

First, get comfortable with saying no and setting boundaries. Women often find themselves engaged in what is termed "office housework," taking on additional responsibilities that do not necessarily contribute to their career advancement. This emotional labor—such as planning office parties or attending to the needs of others—can lead to burnout and resentment. It's crucial for women to get comfortable saying no and setting clear boundaries regarding their roles and responsibilities. Saying yes to everything is saying no to yourself. Learning to prioritize your time and energy is essential, as many women are socialized to be people pleasers, which can further perpetuate inequality and limit their professional growth.

Manage how others view you, as perceptions are key in professional settings. One effective strategy is to take the middle seat in discussions or meetings, where you can assert yourself without being sidelined. By positioning yourself strategically, you can influence conversations and demonstrate your value, which is essential in environments that may not always recognize your contributions. This technique not only helps in maintaining a presence but also allows women to build confidence in their capabilities.

Stop apologizing needlessly for things that are out of your control. Women have a tendency to apologize more often than men.[127] "Sorry, can you send out our call schedule for next week?" "Sorry, can you speak louder?" Certainly, if you are in the wrong or overdue on a report, you should apologize. However, apologizing unnecessarily can be seen as a sign of weakness and can undermine authority. Over-apologizing doesn't send a message of strength. Instead, it minimizes you, your presence, and your contribution. Try to be more direct in your work communications. Being more intentional in how you express yourself will help you be seen as a leader and a trusted authority. By speaking more straightforwardly and clearly, you can showcase your skills and feel more confident in the process.

Get clear on what you want and ask for it. Clarity in your aspirations is vital. We should not assume a no when seeking opportunities; instead, we should articulate what we want and present options that allow others to engage in decision-making. For instance, proposing a series of choices when requesting resources or support can empower the person on the receiving end while still steering the conversation toward the desired outcome. This approach fosters collaboration and enhances the likelihood of achieving personal and professional goals.

Find a mentor and a sponsor. Having both of these within an organization can significantly impact a woman's career trajectory. A mentor is typically someone who has navigated similar challenges and can offer guidance based on their experiences. A sponsor, on the other hand, is someone in a position of influence who can advocate for a woman's promotion or recognition in meetings. Having both a mentor and a sponsor helps to create a support system that enhances visibility and opportunities within the workplace.

Surround yourself with big thinkers. Jim Rohn, self-made millionaire, entrepreneur, author, and motivational speaker, said, "You are the average of the five people you spend the most time with."[128] This statement reflects the research that shows how we are heavily influenced by our relationships and peer groups. Surround yourself with those who uplift you and inspire you to be better.

Celebrate wins, no matter how big they are. Acknowledging wins can keep you positive and build momentum.

Help lift others, especially those behind you. No scarcity here! As you ascend in your career, it's essential to extend a helping hand to those who follow. Amplifying the voices of younger colleagues and mentoring them not only helps to cultivate the next generation of female leaders but also fosters a culture of support and solidarity. By actively participating in each other's success, women can challenge the existing power dynamics and create a more inclusive environment where everyone can thrive.

Finally, be the heroine of your own story! You get to live this one crazy life, and you should live it your way. Be brave. Dream big. Take action. If you dream of a fair world, where women are reimbursed at the same pay as men, women are promoted based on potential like men, and no gender bias exists, I commend you. I am with you. At first blush, this seems too monumental to do. But if we look at how far women have already come and the gains we have made over the last decades instead of thinking about how big the gaps still are, we can be encouraged. In the 1970s an employer could fire a woman for being pregnant, and women were not allowed to hold personal credit cards unless their husbands cosigned. Certainly, women's rights have come a long way since then, but there is still room to go. Sweeping cultural changes do not occur overnight but rather slowly, over time, with individuals like Rosa Parks, Malala Yousafzai, and Ruth Bader Ginsburg, each acting out in their own way to make their dreams come true and set a path for others to build upon. So can you. Individually we can make a difference and create change, one person at a time. Collectively we can change the workplace for future generations of women to come.

CONCLUSION

TIDYING UP

"Appreciation can make a day, even change a life. Your willingness to put it into words is all that is necessary."
—WIDELY ATTRIBUTED TO MARGARET COUSINS

I worried that writing my account would never amount to much. I would say to myself, "No one is going to want to read my story." I worried that I would, once again, "get in trouble" for writing this. I would be called to the proverbial principal's office. (Catholic guilt and fear still reign large in my psyche.)

I worried that it wouldn't be perfect. I wouldn't get everything right.

My chapters never seemed good enough, never encapsulated all I wanted to say. There's always room for improvement. It's not like math or science, where there is just one answer, plain and simple. So I was worried and frozen in fear.

But then, it happened. I decided it didn't matter. This book was for me and for anyone who it might possibly help. It didn't need to be perfect.

I love this mantra, widely attributed to Voltaire, and I try to embrace it: "Perfect is the enemy of good." So I just started writing.

* * *

I noticed over the intervening, liminal (nod to my daughter Ellis who introduced me to this term) months that I had softened. I was tired of so much anger and hurt. I wanted to start over. Yes, I was wronged. Yes, there are system problems—huge ones. Licking my wounds and ruminating over all that I had lost was not letting me see all that I had gained.

I gained my life back. I was no longer crying myself to sleep. It had been months since then. I was no longer walking on eggshells, wondering when I would be summoned for another ambush attack. I was no longer dreading getting up in the morning. This was huge! I had my life back. I could sleep in, catch up on all the streaming series I missed along the way (hello, *Suits*, *Bridgerton*, even *The Sopranos*). I could go to my daughter's track meets and host team dinners. I could walk the dogs midday in the sunshine and run into neighbors, who were shocked by my mere daylight presence. I could meet up for coffee with friends and other colleagues who were retired, something I had never done my whole adult life.

I was free of the constraints of a toxic environment, able to refuel my energy and begin to dream of what was next. But before moving forward, I wanted to ensure I "cleaned up" the past. My kids always joke that what I love to do the most, if I have time, is clean. Not really, but I do love things in order.

So I had to get my house in order.

Not literally. Our house was fine.
Figuratively.

* * *

I want to apologize to all those who suffered with me, especially in the last five years.

Mainly, my husband, Chris. Countless nights listening to the ins and outs of the happenings at work. Faceless names he heard over the years of people he would never encounter but who impacted me (and thus him) daily. He listened. He counseled. He let me cry. He was there. Not an easy task at times, but he was.

I know at times I was not the best wife or mom either. Distracted in my own head at times, maybe present physically but perhaps absent mentally. I have carried trauma responses and unhealthy ways of looking at things into our daily lives. Overanalyzing to see how I am getting the raw end of the deal—something that defies the concert of giving those the benefit of the doubt and a loving household. I know I was short-tempered. But I have learned to give myself grace.

Grace to accept that I was human, doing the best I could. To deal with the worst situation I have had to deal with in my entire life. And I have come out of it. I survived. Battered and wounded but whole.

I'm not sure if this was the right approach, but I shielded the kids from what was happening. They obviously knew when I came home from work upset and crying. They obviously knew something was up, but I never shared the stories. I felt they were too young, too innocent. I didn't want to jade them. As my oldest, my daughter, Ellis, grew up, I peppered female empowerment lessons in. My boys and youngest were always within earshot. They received some education, I suppose, but do not know the whole story.

It's time to share with them too.

Part of the tidying things up before moving on.

AFTERWORD

2025

"Look closely at the present you are constructing: it should look like the future you are dreaming."
—WIDELY ATTRIBUTED TO ALICE WALKER

This book has taken me a lot longer to complete than I initially thought it would. But here we are, in a new era. I would be remiss if I did not address what seems like the proverbial gigantic elephant looming in the room waiting to stomp on all the forward strides women's rights have made in past years.

The day was Monday, January 20, 2025.

That's a day to remember! Not only was it the second time a president was inaugurated for a second, nonconsecutive term (Grover Cleveland was the only other, for all you *Jeopardy!* players and trivia buffs), but it was a day marking the first time a convicted felon took the oath of office. Certainly I am no political expert and do not want to turn this book into a political commentary, but let's just say on that day, there were lots of feelings on both sides of the political spectrum. Some were exuberant that a man who many believe had his second term stolen from him was reinstated to "Make America Great Again." Others mourned what they imagined would be a rolling back of rights for already marginalized groups.

The Trump Administration's second term began with a flurry of administrative announcements and signing a series of executive orders aimed at dismantling DEI initiatives within federal agencies. These orders placed DEI staff on administrative leave and even compiled watch lists of federal employees engaged in equity efforts. Companies including hospitals began to take away years' worth of diversity, equity, and inclusivity work: websites, protocols, and initiatives around inclusive language were erased, so as to not be met with investigations and withholding of federal funding.

So what does this mean for women in the workplace? It means more hurdles, less help, and no clear office with resources aimed at helping them. It means leveling the playing field will be harder. It means that instead of a hired administrator calling for fairness and proactively initiating programs to help, it will be everyone's job to do so as well as the hospital administration.

My hope for this book was to raise awareness around discriminatory practices and biases, whether unconscious or conscious. As individuals, we can all reflect on our own perceptions and whether they are rooted in age-old chauvinistic expectations or biases. Are we part of the problem? We can examine how we address women in meetings—as examples, do we interrupt? Do we make assumptions about whether a woman may want an advancement based on whether she just had a child? Or, conversely, are we part of the solution? Do we amplify her voice and redirect conversation back to her when she is interrupted? Do we nominate her for advancement? We can all do our part.

I contend that workplaces do not need to operate under a DEI flag to create fairness, and certainly we will need to embrace this concept even more now. It is imperative that we do not lose ground and go backward. Even without DEI offices, hospitals, physician groups, and companies can still work toward creating more equitable workspaces. As a system, administration can set up practices that demand open advertisement of positions and transparent processes for promotion and tenure. No behind-closed-doors shuffling of positions to besties to help them get ahead while leaving others behind. No more locker room deals worked out between tennis buddies, allowing friends to advance while others are left wondering how that new job was filled when it wasn't even posted.

Evidence exists that shows how diverse workforces, diverse C-suites, and diverse boards perform better (refer to Chapter 8). Having different viewpoints at the table allows for a more robust conversation around the needs of an organization, opportunities to grow, and different perspectives needed for a global market. When an organization all looks and thinks the same, opportunities are lost; yet many times, hiring committees are looking for that "cultural fit." This "cultural fit," which often means they look the same, like the same hobbies, and think the same, often leads to very homogeneous workplaces and leaves minorities, including women, out. To eliminate some of these biases of hiring for "cultural fit," having structured interview questions and scoring rubrics can take some subjectivity out of hiring practices. Embedding organizational decision-making into transparent frameworks allows inclusivity to be a real hallmark of the culture of a company and not just a banner or buzzword used in propaganda.

I touched on NDAs a bit earlier but as a brief recall, when someone does face harassment or discrimination in the workplace, they are often held to NDAs. Statistics state that over one-third of all workers in America have an NDA already in place when they accept a job.[129] NDAs were initially intended to prevent employees from stealing proprietary information regarding their companies' work products. They were not intended to protect criminal behavior and prevent victims from speaking out. If NDAs regarding conduct or illegal behavior witnessed on the job were not enforceable or permitted, companies would have to do more to ensure those behaviors did not exist in the first place. They would have to protect their employees from encountering this rather than protecting themselves from having the behavior exposed. Holding companies accountable when they fall short in protecting their employees would also raise the bar for faster equity in the workspace. There is legislation out now, and many are working hard for this. Get involved!

The most recent example of an NDA being leveled against an employee who is speaking out about toxic workplace situations is the legal fight between Sarah Wynn-Williams and Meta. In her book, *Careless People: A Cautionary Tale of Power, Greed, and Lost Idealism*, she exposes her experiences working at Meta. An Amazon book review states that in her memoir she touches on "misogyny and double standards behind the scenes" and the horrible culture at Meta. Mark Zuckerberg is unhappy with this exposé for obvious reasons and has had his legal team win an emergency ruling stopping Wynn-Williams from promoting or distributing her book on the grounds that it violates an NDA clause in her severance agreement.[130] Ironically, his legal fight to uphold the NDA has probably brought more publicity to the book and increased its exposure.

I, too, have had trepidation in writing this book. I fear that I will be sued and have to face more legal wranglings. I certainly do not want that. After five years of legal meetings, briefs, and bills, I certainly do not want to be on the receiving end of a lawsuit because of sharing my life story. I have taken great pains to shield the identity of those whose actions have been the basis of some of what I encountered. I have not mentioned names or places. But I also cannot erase twenty-four years of my life. I cannot, and will not, act as if those years and experiences did not happen. Unfortunately, they did happen. I wish they did not. I wish I never had the fodder for this book and that none of the events of the past years happened. But they did. We as a society need to recognize that until equity in the workplace exists, we are stifling potential, losing opportunities, and truly not reaching our individual or collective potential.

We cannot erase the past, all the hurdles all women have had to overcome, but we need to acknowledge that it happened and learn from it. For as George Santayana wrote, "Those who cannot remember the past are condemned to repeat it."

My hope is that this book has created a backdrop for others to see what obstacles women face, whether these obstacles are intentionally placed or not. For people to see how words matter, how little jokes can sting instead of be funny, and how decisions, carelessly made or not, impact others and can have lasting ripple effects.

For all the women out there struggling in their workplaces, know that you are not alone. Unfortunately, millions of women before you and coexisting with you share in your hurdles.

Unfortunately, no superhero is coming to save you. You must be your own hero, or heroine, in your own story. Be brave. Be emboldened, and forge ahead.

ACKNOWLEDGMENTS

"When we focus on our gratitude, the tide of disappointment goes out and the tide of love rushes in."
—WIDELY ATTRIBUTED TO KRISTIN ARMSTRONG

John Donne said it well: "No man is an island," and no woman is an island either.

I have drawn strength and support from many throughout my life, and all my accomplishments have been because of the love and support I have shared with others. One of the biggest truths I still hold onto comes from my mother. She married my dad almost right after high school and immediately began growing our family. She was high school educated and was the fiercest advocate for education. She regularly stated, "The best way to get ahead is with an education." She kept the home fires burning, with the help of my maternal grandmother, "Nana," while my father worked two jobs and put himself through college.

My mother's words certainly hit home, as my oldest brother has a PhD in educational psychology, my two older sisters have a nursing degree and a JD, and I have my MD. Education uplifts!

My dad, who personified hard work and dedication to his family, is a shining example of success, and for everything he did and still does, I am truly grateful.

To my beloved Chris, a.k.a. Stinky. You are a relentless believer in me and have always shown me unconditional support and love. You would traipse four kids down the turnpike to visit me and grab a quick bite while I was on call. You learned how to do crazy girl hairstyles and get all four mobilized in the mornings for school, as I was already out the door by 6:00 a.m. Your ability to believe in me and everyone around you is one of the bazillion reasons people flock to you. (It's also why the kids hate going to the store with you because a simple five-minute trip will turn into an hour, as you know everyone you run into!)

My children have always been my greatest joy: Ellis, Frazier, Harry, and Tessa. They leave me in awe and wonder. I am so lucky to have a front-row seat to watch how these amazing human beings become who they are. They inspire me to be better: a better listener, a better mom, a better person, even a better runner! It always amazes me that even though all four come from the same genetic pool and have the same foundational experiences, they are so different. Every day, week, month, and year is better than the last. I thank them for their patience and love, for their understanding all the nights I was on call and missed bedtime or an event. I thank them for unconditionally loving me and letting me live vicariously through them. And for their willingness to play Rummy, Skip-Bo, or Qwirkle with me!

A huge acknowledgment goes to my daughter Ellis, whose help and patience any time I asked for assistance with this book was always cheerfully given. Ellis just graduated from Barnard College last May, and as she likes to point out, she graduated with a degree in a language she was already fluent in, English! Thankfully, writing comes easily to her, and I await her first novel someday! She truly has a gift. Little did she know that her first "job" after her summer camp counselor job was to be my editor. She rose to the challenge and dove right in. I cannot thank her enough for her help. Her knowledge of footnoting and Canva graphics is way beyond my abilities, and she has made this book so much better than it was without her.

To my legal team that constantly believed in me and had my back. They understood the toll this had on me and my family and continued to fight the fight for not just me but for all women and marginalized groups. They got it and dispelled the gaslighting that often fell upon me.

I have included a chapter of resources that I have used and found helpful. There are many books, articles, podcasts, and coaches that have helped me through my journey. I have listed some of them and want to thank them for all the work they are doing to help women and bring to light the many issues women must face daily by virtue of just being women. We need the research, knowledge, and voices of these trailblazing women to continue to educate others and carve out new paths for us.

I do not wish to pit women against men. We are all in this together, and I truly believe we will not achieve equity till we work together. There are many men I have encountered in my life and professional journey who have treated me as a true colleague and with the utmost respect. I want to thank them and tell them that their friendship and working with them makes me know there is hope.

And to my fellow women physicians and professionals all forging ahead in these crazy male-dominated fields: I see you. I want you to feel seen and know that you can do it. You can be the change we all need and make a difference. Let's support each other and embolden each other to create the change the world needs. One step at a time!

FRAMEWORKS AND CONCEPTS INDEX

Organized by order of chronological appearance.

IDEA	DEFINITION	EXAMPLE
Unconscious Bias	Implicit attitudes or stereotypes that affect understanding, actions, and decisions in an unconscious manner.	During a grand rounds presentation, a female doctor's achievements and research are summarized in terms of her "helpful" or "supportive" contributions to a project, while a male doctor's are highlighted with emphasis on his "leadership" and "visionary" skills.
Gender Stereotyping	Overgeneralized beliefs about behaviors, roles, or traits associated with a specific gender.	Assuming women are warm caregivers while assuming men are strong leaders.

IDEA	DEFINITION	EXAMPLE
The Cycle of Male Privilege	The reinforcing loop where men dominate leadership and decision-making roles, excluding women and perpetuating inequity.	A male physician prioritizes male friends and colleagues for promotions, maintaining a male-dominated leadership structure.
Role Incredulity	A form of gender bias where women are mistakenly assumed to be in support or stereotypically female roles.	Patients assume that the woman in scrubs walking into the room is the nurse instead of the doctor.
Tall Poppy Syndrome	The tendency to criticize or undermine individuals (especially women) who achieve success or stand out.	A female physician earns her "doctor" title after years of rigorous training, yet colleagues refer to her as "Emma" in front of patients or jokingly as "Princess" in their office. Patients and colleagues alike don't respect her as knowledgeable and qualified even though she went through the same training as her male peers.
The Male Blueprint	A set of workplace norms and expectations that prioritize traits traditionally linked to masculinity (such as assertiveness and competitiveness), disadvantaging women who are less likely to be perceived as possessing these traits and exhibiting these behaviors.	A female medical student is passed up from matching into a hospital because they took her male classmate. They both have taken the same classes and worked in the same lab. However, he is perceived as a stronger candidate because the hospital is looking for someone who is assertive and ready to take control of the situation. His letter of recommendation highlights these qualities, unlike hers.
Emotional Labor	The effort to manage emotions and provide emotional support in a professional setting, often disproportionately expected of women.	A female doctor is expected to soothe patients' anxieties while her male counterparts focus solely on clinical tasks.

IDEA	DEFINITION	EXAMPLE
Gendered Division of Labor	The unequal allocation of responsibilities on the basis of gender, which applies to the workplace and in the household.	Male workers assume colleague Charlotte will bake brownies for their meeting and organize the holiday party. A husband expects his wife will cook dinner and watch the kids after they have both had a full day of work.
Double Bind	The contradictory expectations placed on women, where fulfilling one role leads to criticism in another.	A female doctor is seen as too aggressive if assertive and too weak if empathetic.
Mommy Guilt	The emotional burden working mothers feel when trying to balance professional and family responsibilities.	A female physician feels guilty for working long hours instead of spending time with her children.
Maternal Wall	The biases and barriers mothers face in the workplace, such as being perceived as less committed or competent.	A female surgeon asks for a room for her case and is accused of wanting to get out sooner "so she can get home to her children." In her colleagues' eyes, her personal life always takes priority over her professional life.
Benevolent Sexism	Attitudes or behaviors that seem positive or protective but actually reinforce gender stereotypes or inequality.	A male doctor invites his male colleagues to play golf this weekend but doesn't invite his female colleague because he doesn't think she would enjoy the activity and doesn't want her to feel uncomfortable. She misses out on networking and team bonding, impacting her career growth.

IDEA	DEFINITION	EXAMPLE
Hostile Sexism	Overtly negative attitudes or behavior toward women, often to assert dominance or control.	The exclusion of a woman from meetings to reduce her influence in the group, commenting on the way her scrubs fit, sending sexually charged emails, or demoting her from a position after a disagreement.
Sunk Cost Fallacy	Continuing a course of action because of prior investment, even if it's detrimental.	A female doctor stays in a toxic workplace because she has worked for years to accomplish this dream.
Toxic Masculinity	Behavior driven by rigid, traditional notions of masculinity (such as dominance, aggression, violence, and emotional suppression), which fosters a hostile or exclusionary environment.	A male doctor's parent just died. After taking the allocated time off work to attend the funeral and spend time with family, he returns to work but struggles to perform at his usual capacity. His male boss is unsympathetic and tells him, "Get over it already. You're a doctor, not some emotional wreck. Patients need you to man up and focus."
Scarcity Mindset	The belief that opportunities are limited, leading to competition rather than collaboration, especially among women.	Two new seats are open on a board, with one male physician and two female physicians under consideration. The two female candidates, assuming the board would never choose both of them, begin sabotaging each other at work. (In this hypothetical scenario, the board isn't inherently biased toward men and is fully open to hiring both women.)

IDEA	DEFINITION	EXAMPLE
Tokenism	Superficial efforts to appear inclusive by appointing a small number of women or minorities without real change.	A twelve-person board elects one woman (or other minority demographic) to "represent (the entirety of) the female perspective." Now the board can say, "Look! We value women. We have one on the board!"
Internalized Misogyny	When women adopt sexist attitudes or behaviors against other women or themselves.	A female physician questions another woman's competence more harshly than she would a man's.
Shine Theory	The idea that women are stronger and more successful when they support each other rather than compete.	Two female doctors advocate for each other in leadership meetings to ensure equal opportunities.
Hepeating	When a man repeats a woman's idea and takes credit for it, often gaining recognition she was denied.	A male physician receives praise for a treatment suggestion originally made by a female colleague.
Gaslighting	Manipulative behavior aimed at making someone question their perception or memory of events.	A male boss tells a female doctor she's overreacting to sexist comments, making her doubt her experience.

EXTENDED READING

I wanted to include a list of all the amazing women whose work helped me understand my own experiences. I hope to build a community of like-minded, empowered women and provide a space where we can uplift each other's work instead of being pitted against each other.

Caroline Criado Perez wrote an incredible book called *Invisible Women: Data Bias in a World Designed for Men* that discusses how the world has been designed by and for men. She brings to light how systems are constructed and designed to cater to men while women are stuck in the margins. The thoughts in her book helped me conceptualize how systemic inequality affects women in the world and how it applies to the medical field as well as the world at large.

Aminatou Sow and **Ann Friedman** coined the term "shine theory" as a way to think about uplifting and supporting others. They are cohosts of the podcast *Call Your Girlfriend*. You can learn more about shine theory at their website or in Chapter 4 of their book *Big Friendship: How We Keep Each Other Close*.

Mikaela Kiner wrote the book *Female Firebrands: Stories* *and Techniques to Ignite Change, Take Control, and Succeed in the Workplace.* This book shares the stories of thirteen women professionals and discusses how women can overcome workplace challenges. She also wrote an article in the *Harvard Business Review* titled "It's Time to Break the Cycle of Female Rivalry," about how women can support other women.

Rachel Minkin, PhD, and **Juliana Menasce Horowitz, PhD,** published a report with the Pew Research Center called "Parenting in America Today" about recent trends (2020–2022) regarding gendered responsibilities, the division of labor, and the evolving expectations parents hold for their children's futures.

Gretchen Carlson and **Julie Roginsky** are the co-founders of Lift Our Voices, a nonprofit organization that advocates for workers' rights by fighting to end forced arbitration and NDAs.

Here's to all of us ladies.

"Alone we can do so little. Together we can do so much."

—WIDELY ATTRIBUTED TO HELEN KELLER

ABOUT THE AUTHOR

KOLLEEN DOUGHERTY, MD, FASA, is a physician who is double board certified in anesthesiology and critical care medicine. Born and raised in New Jersey, she ventured south for college at Emory University, where she earned a BA in biology and a BA in chemistry. She then went on to Columbia University College of Physicians and Surgeons where she earned her medical degree and worked as an intern in internal medicine. Boston was her next northward destination, where she completed her residency in anesthesiology at the Brigham and Women's Hospital and completed her critical care fellowship at Massachusetts General Hospital.

She practiced in anesthesia and critical care medicine for over two decades at a Level 1 trauma center in New England, where she cared for patients and trained residents and medical students. Kolleen is a member of the American Society of Anesthesiologists and a member of the American Society of Anesthesia Subcommittee on Women. She is also a certified Professional Coach and Life Coach through The Life Coach School.

She has four amazing children: one college graduate, two in college, and her youngest starting college this year. Her days are lovingly filled with her husband of twenty-five years, her two loyal poodles and now a cat, who wandered into their lives one summer night.

She enjoys walks, days on the beach filled with a good beach read, playing board games (sometimes competitively), and just spending time with her family and friends.

This is her first book.

NOTES

1   William H. Chafe, *The Paradox of Change: American Women in the 20th Century* (Oxford University Press, 1991).

2   Malala Yousafzai, speech to the United Nations, July 12, 2013.

3   Amy Zeidan et al., "'Why Bother?': Barriers to Reporting Gender and Sexual Harassment in Emergency Medicine," *Academic Emergency Medicine* 29, no. 9 (September 2022): 1067–77, https://doi.org/10.1111/acem.14544.

4   Stefanie K. Johnson et al., "Why We Fail to Report Sexual Harassment," *Harvard Business Review*, October 4, 2016, https://hbr.org/2016/10/why-we-fail-to-report-sexual-harassment.

5   Nicole Bateman and Martha Ross, "Why Has COVID-19 Been Especially Harmful for Working Women?," Brookings, October 2020, https://www.brookings.edu/articles/why-has-covid-19-been-especially-harmful-for-working-women/.

6   Amy Paturel, "Why Women Leave Medicine," AAMC, October 1, 2019, https://www.aamc.org/news/why-women-leave-medicine.

7   Paturel, "Why Women Leave Medicine."

8   Stuart Heiser, "The Majority of U.S. Medical Students Are Women, New Data Show," AAMC, December 9, 2019, https://www.aamc.org/news/press-releases/majority-us-medical-students-are-women-new-data-show.

9   Zeidan et al., "'Why Bother?': Barriers to Reporting Gender and Sexual Harassment."

10 Zeidan et al., "'Why Bother?': Barriers to Reporting Gender and Sexual Harassment."

11 Johnson et al., "Why We Fail to Report Sexual Harassment."

12 Zeidan et al., "'Why Bother?': Barriers to Reporting Gender and Sexual Harassment."

13 "Dig It! How Oprah's Growing Healthier—and You Can Too," Oprah.com, May 14, 2013, https://www.oprah.com/home/oprahs-maui-farm-oprah-on-growing-her-own-food/all.

14 Simone de Beauvoir, *The Second Sex*, trans. Constance Borde and Sheila Malovany-Chevallier (Éditions Gallimard, 1949; repr., Vintage Books, 2011).

15 Ron Southwick, "Female Doctors Earn $2M Less over Their Careers," Chief Healthcare Executive, December 7, 2021, https://www.chiefhealthcareexecutive.com/view/female-doctors-earn-2m-less-over-their-careers.

16 Ron Southwick, "Women Doctors Are Earning Less Than Men, at All Stages of Their Careers," Chief Healthcare Executive, October 18, 2022, https://www.chiefhealthcareexecutive.com/view/women-doctors-are-earning-less-than-men-at-all-stages-of-their-careers.

17 Saumya Kalia, "Online Doctor Reviews Are Gender Biased, More Likely to Call Women 'Cold': Study," The Swaddle, October 11, 2022, https://www.theswaddle.com/online-doctor-reviews-are-gender-biased-more-likely-to-call-women-cold-study.

18 Kimber P. Richter et al., "Women Physicians and Promotion in Academic Medicine," *New England Journal of Medicine* 383, no. 22 (November 25, 2020): 2148–57, https://doi.org/10.1056/NEJMsa1916935; Jessica A. Gold et al., "Gender Differences in Endowed Chairs in Medicine at Top Schools," *JAMA Internal Medicine* 180, no. 10 (August 2020): 1391–94, https://doi.org/10.1001/jamainternmed.2020.2677; and Beenish Safdar et al., "Gender Disparity in Grants and Awards at the National Institute of Health," *Cureus* 13, no. 4 (April 23, 2021): e14644, https://doi.org/10.7759/cureus.14644.

19 Julie K. Silver et al., "Assessment of Women Physicians Among Authors of Perspective-Type Articles Published in High-Impact Pediatric Journals," *JAMA Network Open* 1, no. 3 (July 20, 2018): e180802, https://doi.org/10.1001/jamanetworkopen.2018.0802; and Sara Reardon, "Fewer Citations for Female Authors of Medical Research," *Nature* (July 29, 2021), https://doi.org/10.1038/d41586-021-02102-8.

20 Shannon M. Ruzycki et al., "Trends in the Proportion of Female Speakers at Medical Conferences in the United States and in Canada, 2007 to 2017," *JAMA Network Open* 2, no. 4 (April 12, 2019): e192103, https://doi.org/10.1001/jamanetworkopen.2019.2103.

21 Pamela W. Henderson and Robert A. Peterson, "Mental Accounting and Categorization," *Organizational Behavior and Human Decision Processes* 51, no. 1 (February 1992): 92–117, https://doi.org/10.1016/0749-5978(92)90006-S.

22 Malcolm Gladwell, *Blink: The Power of Thinking Without Thinking* (Little, Brown, 2005).

23 Erin Carson, "When Tech Firms Judge on Skills Alone, Women Land More Job Interviews," CNET, August 27, 2016, https://www.cnet.com/tech/tech-industry/when-tech-firms-judge-on-skills-alone-women-land-more-job-interviews/.

24 Kelsey Piper, "The Conversation About Diversity in Tech Is Getting Hijacked by Bad Research," *Vox*, February 20, 2019, https://www.vox.com/2019/2/20/18232762/gender-diversity-tech-bad-research-recruiting-new-york-times.

25 "Geena Davis Institute Study Shows Gender Gap in Film/TV Is Prevalent Worldwide," LAist, September 23, 2014, https://laist.com/shows/the-frame/geena-davis-institute-study-shows-gender-gap-in-film-tv-is-prevalent-worldwide.

26 Douglas Broom, "More Women Than Ever Are Working in Hollywood, but Men Still Dominate Key Roles," World Economic Forum, The European Sting, February 16, 2020, https://europeansting.com/2020/02/16/more-women-than-ever-are-working-in-hollywood-but-men-still-dominate-key-roles/.

27 Angelina Fedorova, "Stereotypical Women's Representation in the Film Industry," Arcadia, January 27, 2023, https://www.byarcadia.org/post/stereotypical-women-s-representation-in-the-film-industry.

28 Adrianne Pasquarelli, "The Force Is with Females in 'Star Wars' Marketing This Year," *Ad Age*, September 19, 2016, https://adage.com/article/cmo-strategy/expect-females-star-wars-marketing-year/305885/.

29   Angela Garcia and Savanah Hinojosa, "The Double Standard Revolving Around Taylor Swift and Her Relationships," RTF Gender and Media Culture, July 2, 2022, https://rtfgenderandmediaculture.wordpress.com/2022/07/02/the-double-standard-revolving-around-taylor-swift-and-her-relationships/.

30   "Tracking Gender in the 2020 Presidential Election," Center for American Women and Politics, Rutgers Eagleton Institute of Politics, accessed June 9, 2025, womenrun.rutgers.edu/2020-presidential/.

31   "Current Numbers," Center for American Women and Politics, Rutgers–New Brunswick Eagleton Institute of Politics, accessed November 7, 2024, https://cawp.rutgers.edu/facts/current-numbers.

32   United States Census Bureau, "Explore Census Data," accessed June 9, 2025, https://data.census.gov/.

33   Drew DeSilver and Carrie Blazina, "A Record Number of Women Are Serving in the 117th Congress," Pew Research Center, January 15, 2021, https://www.pewresearch.org/short-reads/2021/01/15/a-record-number-of-women-are-serving-in-the-117th-congress/.

34   Meredith Conroy, "Here's How We Talk About Manhood—and Womanhood—During a Presidential Race," *The Washington Post*, July 27, 2016, https://www.washingtonpost.com/news/monkey-cage/wp/2016/07/27/heres-how-we-talk-about-manhood-and-womanhood-during-a-presidential-race/.

35   Robert L. Helmreich et al., "A Psychometric Analysis of the Personal Attributes Questionnaire," *Sex Roles* 7, no. 11 (1981): 1097–1108, http://dx.doi.org/10.1007/bf00287587; and Leonie Huddy and Nayda Terkildsen, "Gender Stereotypes and the Perception of Male and Female Candidates," *American Journal of Political Science* 37, no. 1 (February 1993): 119–47, https://doi.org/10.2307/2111526.

36   Kate McCarthy, "Name It. Change It.'s New Research Explained by Stick Figures," *Name It. Change It* (blog), April 8, 2013, http://www.nameitchangeit.org/blog/entry/Name-It-Change-Its-New-Research-Explained-By-Stick-Figures.

37   "Are Children's Job Aspirations Defined by Gender?," Michael Page, accessed June 9, 2025, https://www.michaelpage.co.uk/diversity-campaign/childrens-job-aspirations-defined-by-gender.

38   Bryan Stevenson, *Just Mercy: A Story of Justice and Redemption* (Spiegel & Grau, 2014).

39   Emma Greguska, "Study: Female Doctors Less Likely to Be Referred to by Title," Arizona State University News, July 21, 2017, https://news.asu.edu/20170721-solutions-asu-mayo-study-how-female-doctors-introduced.

40   Anita Kumar, "What's in a Name? 'Hillary' by Any Other Name Would Still Be Controversial," *McClatchy DC*, April 7, 2015, https://www.mcclatchydc.com/news/politics-government/election/article24782737.html.

41   Kumar, "What's in a Name?"

42   Kumar, "What's in a Name?"

43   Caitlin Geng, "What to Know About Tall Poppy Syndrome," Medical News Today, June 24, 2024, https://www.medicalnewstoday.com/articles/tall-poppy-syndrome.

44   Geng, "What to Know About Tall Poppy Syndrome."

45   Women of Influence+, "The Cost of Ambition: New Research Finds Almost 90 Percent of Women Worldwide Are Penalized and Undermined Because of Their Achievements at Work," Cision News, March 1, 2023, https://www.newswire.ca/news-releases/the-cost-of-ambition-new-research-finds-almost-90-per-cent-of-women-worldwide-are-penalized-and-undermined-because-of-their-achievements-at-work-859610016.html.

46   Women of Influence+, "The Cost of Ambition."

47   Katie Couric, *Going There* (Little, Brown, 2021).

48. Hope Reese, "What Is Emotional Labor, and Why Does It Matter?," *Greater Good Magazine*, April 5, 2023, https://greatergood.berkeley.edu/article/item/what_is_emotional_labor_and_why_does_it_matter.

49. Linda Babcock et al., "Why Women Volunteer for Tasks That Don't Lead to Promotions," *Harvard Business Review*, July 16, 2018, https://hbr.org/2018/07/why-women-volunteer-for-tasks-that-dont-lead-to-promotions.

50. Associated Press, "Margaret Thatcher Quotes from a Life in Politics," Politico, April 8, 2013, https://www.politico.com/story/2013/04/margaret-thatcher-quotes-from-a-life-in-politics-089742.

51. Parth Shah et al., "The Double Bind for Women in Leadership," *NPR*, March 5, 2018, https://www.npr.org/2018/03/05/590881966/-shes-shrill-but-hes-just-being-a-boss-the-double-bind-for-women-in-leadership.

52. "The Gender Gap at Medical Schools in the United States," Women in Academia Report, December 20, 2023, https://wiareport.com/2023/12/the-gender-gap-at-medical-schools-in-the-united-states/.

53. Silvia Wiesner, "The Male Blueprint: What It Is—and How It Stops Women from Reaching the C-Suite," World Economic Forum, March 8, 2024, https://www.weforum.org/stories/2024/03/the-male-blueprint-what-is-it-and-how-does-it-stop-women-from-reaching-the-c-suite/.

54. Vasiliki Bozani, "Masculinity, Femininity, and Workplace Outcomes," in *Handbook of Labor, Human Resources and Population Economics*, ed. Klaus F. Zimmermann (Springer, 2020), https://doi.org/10.1007/978-3-319-57365-6_24-1.

55. Bozani, "Masculinity, Femininity, and Workplace Outcomes."

56. Tara Sophia Mohr, "Why Women Don't Apply for Jobs Unless They're 100% Qualified," *Harvard Business Review*, August 25, 2014, https://hbr.org/2014/08/why-women-dont-apply-for-jobs-unless-theyre-100-qualified.

57. Colleen Flaherty, "Defying a Gendered 'Narrative,'" Inside Higher Ed, March 8, 2022, https://www.insidehighered.com/news/2022/03/09/study-challenges-gender-bias-letters-recommendation.

58. Flaherty, "Defying a Gendered 'Narrative.'"

59. Kim Elsesser, "College Professors Tried to Reduce Gender Bias in Evaluations—but Couldn't," *Forbes*, October 22, 2024, https://www.forbes.com/sites/kimelsesser/2024/10/22/college-professors-tried-to-reduce-gender-bias-in-evaluations-but-couldnt/.

60. Ronke M. Olabisi, "The Pregnancy Drop: How Teaching Evaluations Penalize Pregnant Faculty," *Humanities and Social Sciences Communications* 8 (October 29, 2021): 253, https://www.nature.com/articles/s41599-021-00926-3.

61. Mallory Locklear, "Black and Women Scientists Are Less Likely to Have Multiple Research Grants," YaleNews, February 28, 2023, https://news.yale.edu/2023/02/28/black-and-women-scientists-are-less-likely-have-multiple-research-grants.

62. Marie Hemingway, "The Unseen Consequences of All-Male Panels (#Manels)," LinkedIn, June 11, 2020, https://www.linkedin.com/pulse/unseen-consequences-all-male-panels-manels-marie-hemingway/?trackingId=38rzHnvgSZGufW%2F%2BAEvO2A%3D%3D.

63. Gloria Lin et al., "The Impact of Gender in Mentor–Mentee Success: Results from the Women's Dermatologic Society Mentorship Survey," *International Journal of Women's Dermatology* 7, no. 4 (September 2021): 398–402, https://doi.org/10.1016/j.ijwd.2021.04.010.

64. Lesley Symons and Herminia Ibarra, "What the Scarcity of Women in Business Case Studies Really Looks Like," *Harvard Business Review*, April 28, 2014, https://hbr.org/2014/04/what-the-scarcity-of-women-in-business-case-studies-really-looks-like.

65 Sumathi Reddy, "In Published Work, Male Scientists Sing Their Own Praises More," *The Wall Street Journal*, December 16, 2019, https://www.wsj.com/articles/in-published-work-male-scientists-sing-their-own-praises-more-11576539053.

66 Eve Rodsky, *Fair Play: A Game-Changing Solution for When You Have Too Much to Do (and More Life to Live)* (G. P. Putnam's Sons, 2019).

67 Richard Fry et al., "In a Growing Share of U.S. Marriages, Husbands and Wives Earn About the Same," Pew Research Center, April 13, 2023, https://www.pewresearch.org/social-trends/2023/04/13/in-a-growing-share-of-u-s-marriages-husbands-and-wives-earn-about-the-same/.

68 Rachel Minkin and Juliana Menasce Horowitz, "Parenting in America Today," Pew Research Center, January 24, 2023, https://www.pewresearch.org/social-trends/2023/01/24/parenting-in-america-today/.

69 Maya Angelou, *Letter to My Daughter* (Random House, 2009).

70 M. Teresa Cardador et al., "Unpacking the Status-Leveling Burden for Women in Male-Dominated Occupations," *Administrative Science Quarterly* 67, no. 1 (August 2021): 237–84, https://doi.org/10.1177/00018392211038505.

71 Dan Pilat and Sekoul Krastev, "The Similar-To-Me Effect," The Decision Lab, accessed June 9, 2025, https://thedecisionlab.com/reference-guide/psychology/the-similar-to-me-effect.

72 "5 Cognitive Biases That Sabotage Gender Diversity in Hiring," Mercer, accessed June 9, 2025, https://www.mercer.com/en-us/insights/talent-and-transformation/diversity-equity-and-inclusion/5-cognitive-biases-that-sabotage-gender-diversity-in-hiring/.

73 Emily Harris, "Misdiagnosis Might Harm up to 800,000 US Patients Annually," *JAMA* 330, no. 7 (2023): 586, https://doi.org/10.1001/jama.2023.13135.

74 Patricia Louie and Rima Wilkes, "Representations of Race and Skin Tone in Medical Textbook Imagery," *Social Science & Medicine* 202 (April 2018): 38–42, https://doi.org/10.1016/j.socscimed.2018.02.023.

75 David Limm, "The Creator of a Viral Black Fetus Medical Illustration Blends Art and Activism," HealthCity, Boston Medical Center, January 13, 2022, https://healthcity.bmc.org/creator-viral-black-fetus-medical-illustration-blends-art-and-activism/.

76 Lance Roller, "Illustrating Change: Diversity in Medical Textbooks," Think Global Health, November 7, 2024, https://www.thinkglobalhealth.org/article/illustrating-change-diversity-medical-textbooks; and Tassia O'Callaghan, "The Reframing Revolution: Making Medicine Diverse," Peanut, May 3, 2022.

77 Carrington Moore et al., "'It's Important to Work with People That Look Like Me': Black Patients' Preferences for Patient-Provider Race Concordance," *Journal of Racial and Ethnic Health Disparities* 10 (November 2022): 2552–64, https://doi.org/10.1007/s40615-022-01435-y.

78 Resa E. Lewiss et al., "Stop Protecting 'Good Guys,'" *Harvard Business Review*, August 1, 2022, https://hbr.org/2022/08/stop-protecting-good-guys.

79 Angela Y. Davis, *Women, Race & Class* (Random House, 1981).

80 Cicero, *On Duties*, trans. Walter Miller (Loeb Classical Library, 1913), 87.

81 Chai R. Feldblum and Victoria A. Lipnic, "Select Task Force on the Study of Harassment in the Workplace," US Equal Employment Opportunity Commission, June 2016, https://www.eeoc.gov/select-task-force-study-harassment-workplace-report-co-chairs-chai-r-feldblum-victoria-lipnic.

82 Feldblum and Lipnic, "Select Task Force on the Study of Harassment in the Workplace."

83 Chamari L. Edirisinghe et al., "Bullied After Blowing the Whistle: An Integrative Literature Review," *Beijing Law Review* 12, no. 4 (December 2021): 1148–62, https://doi.org/10.4236/blr.2021.124059.

84　Andrew Bundy, "The Sunk-Cost Fallacy," Courier Express, October 5, 2023, https://www.thecourierexpress.com/opinion/columns/the-sunk-cost-fallacy/article_bec79386-62ee-11ee-9161-8726ce994996.html.

85　Gloria Steinem, *The Truth Will Set You Free, But First It Will Piss You Off! Thoughts on Life, Love, and Rebellion* (Random House, 2019).

86　Mona Soorma, *Soul Food and Instant Karma: Thoughts for an Inspired Living* (2019).

87　Statistics, Lift Our Voices, accessed June 9, 2025, https://liftourvoices.org/statistics.

88　Ending Forced Arbitration of Sexual Assault and Sexual Harassment Act of 2021, H.R. 4445, 117th Cong. (2022), https://www.congress.gov/bill/117th-congress/house-bill/4445/text; and Speak Out Act, 42 U.S.C. Ch. 164 (2022) (enacted), https://uscode.house.gov/view.xhtml?path=/prelim@@title42/chapter164&edition=prelim.

89　Margaret Drabble, *The Millstone* (Harcourt Brace, 1965).

90　Vinod Menon, "20 Years of the Default Mode Network: A Review and Synthesis," *Neuron* 111, no. 16 (August 2023): 2469–87, https://doi.org/10.1016/j.neuron.2023.04.023.

91　Mary Henderson, "Identifying and Mitigating Aggressive Behavior Among Female Physicians," Daily Bulletin, RSNA, November 29, 2023, https://dailybulletin.rsna.org/db23/index.cfm?pg=23wed10.

92　"2022 National Health Care Governance Survey Report," American Hospital Association, January 24, 2023, https://trustees.aha.org/aha-2022-national-health-care-governance-survey-report.

93　Emma Hinchliffe, "Women CEOs Run 10.4% of Fortune 500 Companies. A Quarter of the 52 Leaders Became CEO in the Last Year," *Fortune*, June 5, 2023, https://fortune.com/2023/06/05/fortune-500-companies-2023-women-10-percent/.

94　Jeanne Sahadi, "Share of Women in C-Suite Roles Falls for First Time in Two Decades, Study Finds," *CNN*, April 5, 2024, https://www.cnn.com/2024/04/05/success/gender-parity-women-corporate-leaders.

95　"The Legacy of Ruth Bader Ginsburg," State of Connecticut, accessed June 9, 2025, https://portal.ct.gov/dcf/spotlight/2020/sept-2020/ruth-bader-ginsberg?language=en_US.

96　Melissa Batchelor Warnke, "Jessica Knoll: It's Time to Stop Pitting Women Against Each Other," *Girlboss* (blog), May 15, 2018, https://girlboss.com/blogs/read/jessica-knoll-on-women-and-competition?srsltid=AfmBOoro8lomONqn-iCN82cCUESoeW9pSnAolkxu5Bd6__tysXbqqzDQ.

97　Aminatou Sow and Ann Friedman, *Big Friendship: How We Keep Each Other Close* (Simon & Schuster, 2020).

98　Madeleine Albright, *Madam Secretary: A Memoir* (Miramax, 2003).

99　Mohr, "Why Women Don't Apply for Jobs Unless They're 100% Qualified."

100　Nancy F. Clark, "Act Now to Shrink the Confidence Gap," *Forbes*, April 28, 2014, https://www.forbes.com/sites/womensmedia/2014/04/28/act-now-to-shrink-the-confidence-gap/.

101　Leslie Shore, "Gal Interrupted, Why Men Interrupt Women and How to Avert This in the Workplace," *Forbes*, January 3, 2017, https://www.forbes.com/sites/womensmedia/2017/01/03/gal-interrupted-why-men-interrupt-women-and-how-to-avert-this-in-the-workplace/.

102　"How Often Are Women Interrupted by Men? Here's What the Research Says," Advisory Board, July 7, 2017, https://www.advisory.com/daily-briefing/2017/07/07/men-interrupting-women.

103 Lindsay Dodgson, "Men Are Getting the Credit for Women's Work Through Something Called 'Hepeating'—Here's What It Means," Business Insider, March 8, 2018, https://www.businessinsider.com/what-is-hepeating-2017-9.

104 Yusuke Tsugawa et al., "Comparison of Hospital Mortality and Readmission Rates for Medicare Patients Treated by Male vs Female Physicians," *JAMA Internal Medicine* 177, no. 2 (February 1, 2017): 206–213, https://doi.org/10.1001/jamainternmed.2016.7875; James Cook, "Research Shows Companies with Female CEOs Are More Profitable," Business Leader, September 29, 2022, https://businessleader.co.uk/content/article/49/Research-shows-companies-with-female-CEOs-are-more-profitable; and Erika Christie Berle et al., "Effect of Gender Composition of Committees," *Human Relations* 77, no. 5 (2023): 622–49, https://doi.org/10.1177/00187267221135846.

105 Emma Watson, "Gender equality not only liberates women but also men from prescribed gender stereotypes. #heforshe," Twitter, August 18, 2014, https://x.com/EmmaWatson/status/501467746602061824.

106 Patrick Boyle, "More Women Than Men Are Enrolled in Medical School," AAMC, December 9, 2019, https://www.aamc.org/news/more-women-men-are-enrolled-medical-school.

107 Jason Lesnick, "Leaving So Soon? Why Women Are Retiring from EM Early," JournalFeed, July 18, 2023, https://journalfeed.org/article-a-day/2023/leaving-so-soon-why-women-are-retiring-from-em-early/.

108 Amy Paturel, "Why Women Leave Medicine," AAMC, October 1, 2019, https://www.aamc.org/news/why-women-leave-medicine.

109 Tim Dall et al., *The Complexities of Physician Supply and Demand: Projections from 2019 to 2034* (AAMC, June 2021), https://digirepo.nlm.nih.gov/master/borndig/9918417887306676/9918417887306676.pdf.

110 Andis Robeznieks, "Doctor Shortages Are Here—and They'll Get Worse If We Don't Act Fast," American Medical Association, April 13, 2022, https://www.ama-assn.org/practice-management/sustainability/doctor-shortages-are-here-and-they-ll-get-worse-if-we-don-t-act.

111 Robert Hart, "Patients Fare Better with Women Doctors, Study Finds," *Forbes*, April 22, 2024, https://www.forbes.com/sites/roberthart/2024/04/22/patients-fare-better-with-women-doctors-study-finds/.

112 Tsugawa et al., "Comparison of Hospital Mortality and Readmission Rates for Medicare Patients Treated by Male vs Female Physicians."

113 Hart, "Patients Fare Better with Women Doctors."

114 Talya Miron-Shatz et al., "Physician Experience Is Associated with Greater Underestimation of Patient Pain," *Patient Education and Counseling* 103, no. 2 (February 2020): 405–409, https://doi.org/10.1016/j.pec.2019.08.040.

115 Caroline Surchat et al., "Impact of Physician Empathy on Patient Outcomes: A Gender Analysis," *British Journal of General Practice* 72, no. 715 (2022): e99–107, https://doi.org/10.3399/bjgp.2021.0193.

116 Christopher J. D. Wallis et al., "Association of Surgeon-Patient Sex Concordance with Postoperative Outcomes," *JAMA Surgery* 157, no. 2 (2022): 146–56, https://doi.org/10.1001/jamasurg.2021.6339.

117 Atsushi Miyawaki et al., "Comparison of Hospital Mortality and Readmission Rates by Physician and Patient Sex," *Annals of Internal Medicine* 177, no. 5 (April 23, 2024): 598–608, https://doi.org/10.7326/M23-3163.

118 David Weill, "The Evidence Shows Women Make Better Doctors. So Why Do Men Still Dominate Medicine?," *Los Angeles Times*, October 4, 2024, https://www.latimes.com/opinion/story/2024-10-04/women-doctor-medicine-healthcare-sexism-equality.

119 Christopher J. D. Wallis et al., "Surgeon Sex and Long-Term Postoperative Outcomes Among Patients Undergoing Common Surgeries," *Jama Surgery* 158, no. 11 (2023): 1185–94, https://doi.org/10.1001/jamasurg.2023.3744; and Nikki Dobrin, "New Studies Suggest Female Doctors Make Better Surgeons Than Male Doctors," *People*, August 31, 2023, https://people.com/new-study-suggests-female-doctors-make-better-surgeons-than-male-doctors-7964595.

120 Samantha DiGrande, "Women More Likely to Survive Heart Attacks When Treated by Female Physicians," *AJMC*, August 31, 2018, https://www.ajmc.com/view/women-more-likely-to-survive-heart-attacks-when-treated-by-female-physicians.

121 Katherine A. Fowler et al., "Suicide Among Males Across the Lifespan: An Analysis of Differences by Known Mental Health Status," *American Journal of Preventive Medicine* 63, no. 3 (September 2022): 419–22, https://doi.org/10.1016/j.amepre.2022.02.021.

122 Weill, "The Evidence Shows Women Make Better Doctors."

123 Miyawaki et al., "Comparison of Hospital Mortality and Readmission Rates by Physician and Patient Sex."

124 Elizabeth Pratt, "People Treated by Female Doctors Tend to Have Better Health Outcomes, Study Finds," Medical News Today, April 22, 2024, https://www.medicalnewstoday.com/articles/people-treated-by-female-doctors-tend-to-have-better-health-outcomes-study-finds.

125 Tererai Trent, *The Awakened Woman: A Guide for Remembering & Igniting Your Sacred Dreams* (Enliven Books, 2018).

126 Joanna Barsh and Lareina Yee, *Unlocking the Full Potential of Women at Work* (McKinsey & Company, 2012).

127 Karina Schumann and Michael Ross, "Why Women Apologize More Than Men: Gender Differences in Thresholds for Perceiving Offensive Behavior," *Psychological Science* 21, no. 11 (2010): 1649–55, https://doi.org/10.1177/0956797610384150.

128 Catherine Plano, "You Are the Average of the Five People You Spend Time With," Ellevate, accessed June 9, 2025, https://www.ellevatenetwork.com/articles/9895-you-are-the-average-of-the-five-people-you-spend-time-with.

129 "Petition to End NDAs That Cover Up Toxic Workplace Issues," Lift Our Voices, accessed June 9, 2025, https://liftourvoices.org/petition.

130 Michelle Goldberg, "The Tell-All Book That Meta Doesn't Want You to Read," *The New York Times*, March 17, 2025, https://www.nytimes.com/2025/03/17/opinion/facebook-meta-careless-people.html.